e.q.

Scott Shaw

Buddha Rose Publications

First Printing 1988

ISBN: 1-877792-07-1
ISBN-13: 9781877792076

Library of Congress Catalog Card Number:
2010932184

4 3 2 11 10 9 8 7 6 5

Printed in the United States of America

2

_____ **e.q.**

contents

_e.q._

There was an _e.q._ in L.A. today. 6.1 on the _Gutenberg-Richter Scale_ was the last figure that I heard. So, it wasn't too small by any accounts. Though I have known larger.

It hit a bit after 7:00 AM.

Funny, I once planned on starting a band with the name, _"7:00 AM."_ I wrote the songs, had the full-on concept. But... It went by the wayside. The other member not believing. In his universally negative way saying, _"We'll never get anywhere..."_

But then, there is a lot of things I have had the idea to do but not the support to get it accomplished.

For the record and for the _whatever it is worth..._ I had it planned to be a two-man team. Me on guitar and drum machine, him on the bass. We were going to go with the beatnik vibe: black turtlenecks, black berets, and goatees. The hook, if you want to call it that, is that I came up with the idea to have a mannequin sitting behind a drum kit. We would, of course, talk to him and about him as if he were an actual member of the band.

We did a few rehearsals at my pad when I was living in Manhattan Beach. They went really well as I had written some very cool songs for the concept. But, my friend's focus had changed from the days when we used to play music together back in high school. He no longer had the time or the desire to believe/to hope.

You know, I have long realized that the primary reason people do not succeed is that they do not try. If you try, at least you have accomplished something. If you do not try, then there is no hope of reaching your goals/your dream. Anyway... Back to the story at hand.

*   *   *

I was sleeping when it hit. It was in the morning—the early morning.

I woke to the rumbling. I felt the noise, heard the sound, and knew...

For a moment, a second or two, *but the seconds seem like hours in moments of intensity,* I thought to just lay there in bed; do nothing. What could I do? But it—it continued. The reaffirming motion. And then, the crash of books from my living room bookshelf hitting the ground—hitting something. Convincing me that my bed, as finely Italian as it is, was not the place to be. So, I got up in the seconds that feel like hours.

I searched for clothing as the rumbling continued. What did I have on last evening? Where were they? What part of the floor had I thrown them upon?

I saw my tennis shoes, *New Balance* in a world that now had no balance.

But, the name, a reminder, a symbolic indication to me—a message, as I had wore them in the Philippines, Thailand, and Japan, last winter. I thought. I questioned. Then, the rumbling, it stopped. The pounding of my heart did not.

I saw my clothes: the baggy brown pants, the orangeish print, long sleeve shirt, which had accompanied me to Tibet a few months ago. I put them on.

I stood there not knowing what to do. What does one do? I don't know? When earth and destiny takes hold; the dream, the illusion turns to nothing.

I walked into my living room. I looked and saw several books, all by Bukowski, laying atop the head of my Buddha statue. The statue which I have had for so many years. The statue which holds all of the *malas,* rosaries, and prayer beads which I have collected from around the world.

I saw it, my Buddha, with his head broken wide open from the weight—the impact of the falling Bukowski books. I laughed to myself. Though I loved my Buddha, I thought, *"It is some how poetic that the books written by Bukowski would find their way down to break the head of Mr. Buddha."*

Bukowski and the Buddha, now broken.

*   *   *

With my clothing on and the shaking stopped, I stood there looking. Just than, the shaking reoccurred—an *aftershock.* Once again, I was lost in the world of, *"What to do?"*

The *aftershock,* it slowly found its way into oblivion.

I walked to my front door; opened it. I looked down the hall of my apartment complex. I wondered, *"Was I the only one in the building,"* as there was no movement. I closed the door, thought to put on my *New Balance 1300* tennis shoes, (the one's I saw laying on the floor), without socks and make a B-line for the outside. But, where would I go? Where could 1 go? So, I opened my living room drapes, pushed the glass door farther open, and looked out and onto Hermosa Beach.

The divine mother ocean was still in place, moving to her motion of contentment,

10

where nothing could affect her. For any raindrop falling into her, becomes part-and-parcel of the whole.

There were people out there. Out there on *The Strand.* They were standing in front of their homes. Some sat on their walls—some spoke. I could see them. I could not hear what they had to say. But, at least they were there. It was not, *The Rapture,* where all the holy had been sucked up to heaven, leaving only me, the unholy, left here on this earth all alone.

I sat down on Mr. Couch, grabbed the remote control and turned on the T.V. I flipped through all the local stations but to my amazement, there were no *Special Reports* going down. MTV was still music *video-izing* but no info.

I left the T.V. the on and walked out onto my patio. Looking around, looking at the ocean, looking at the houses on *The Strand,* then looking up, I notice my neighbor—two floors above. He's the one who makes weird chanting noises at the strangest hours for no apparent reasons. Is it opera? I don't know? But, he was out on his balcony and he says,

"Pretty scary, huh?"
"Yeah, but at least it doesn't look like a tsunami is headed our direction."

"A what?"

At this point, my neighbor directly above my apartment comes out on his balcony.

"God, that was scary. I didn't know whether to run outside or what. This is my first earthquake."
The third floor neighbor says, *"Fuck, I was ready to jump. This was my first earthquake too."*
I ask, *"So, you guys aren't from California?"*
"No," came ringing in twice.

Me, I felt proud to be the only local. I mean hey, *Locals Only,* and all that…
I looked and almost had to laugh. Here we were, three guys; one above the other. The only people out on our balconies/patios respectively, in this very large apartment building that spans across the entire beach.
Me, I stood on my larger, lower patio. They stood on their smaller balconies.
Here we are; they were both blonde, and I am blonde. Three blonde guys, outside. One above the other.
They both had tans and short hair. Me, I prefer pale, and my *do* is long. There

we were; same place, but of different worlds.

Yuppies in modern terminology, is what they would/could be called. Which reminds me of a time maybe eleven years ago. There I was longhaired, bearded, a *kurta,* (India shirt), draw string pants, barefooted, walking to the local supermarket for the yoga institute that I belonged to. These two girls pull up, as I stood at the stoplight. They pull up in their *out-of-state* tourist type car and asked,

"Are you a hippie?"
"No", I said, *"I'm a yogi."*

The light changed; I walked on, they drove on—never to be seen again. Upon my return and my recollection of the events to my yoga institute friends, they said,

"See, God was testing you brother."

So, *yuppie...* No, I am nowhere near. They are above: short hair, they both wore, short pants, and a tee-shirt. Me... Well, my clothing was Italian. And, though my guise may have changed over the years, my test is still the same. I am still who I have always been. Been inside. Not necessarily outside.

"Have you been watching T.V.?" asks the third floor *yuppie* neighbor, *"It is more scary than the actually quake."*

We all hesitate and soon the movement was in. First, the middle blonde, probably blue eyed, *yuppie.* Then, the third floor, blue eyed, blonde; in. I am left alone looking at the divine mother ocean, feeling her presence, seeing her morning, and embracing the early morning haze of this autumn day.

As I walk inside, I was thinking to myself, *"Yuppies, this whole building is filled with 'em."*

Once again, I wondered why I lived here. But then, the sound of the ocean caressed my ear and the question faded from my mind.

*   *   *

Some call the beach *yuppies,* *"Buppies."* I prefer that term for black *yuppies,* however. And, *yappies,* that's for the women *yuppies.* And, *gouppies,* that's for the Asian *yuppies.*

Guppies, those are either the rocks a dude shoots off or a fish. Well, with that and all the generalized definitions out of the way...

*   *   *

I went back inside and found a *Special Report* on T.V. It was, surprisingly, only on one station. The other two network giants were still in the mode of the early morning talk shows from New York. As I watched, I noticed that additional books had fallen from the other side of my top bookshelf.

Just for the record, so you can visually recount the issue, I have a lot of books... My bookshelves extend the entire wall of my living room—floor to ceiling. The wall over there—over there by the T.V.

But, back to the storyline...

I found about six or eight R. Buckminster Fuller books had found their way down on top of my VCR'S and had knocked them back into the wall, off of the top of my T.V. I moved the VCR'S back into place.

The books, I stacked one atop the other on a lower shelf—to prevent future falling.

As I went about my business, the newscaster keep speaking of how this may have been the, *"Big One."* Or, was this just the predecessor to the, *"Big One,"* which may be coming at any moment.

I sat there watching the T.V.

Watching: one white, one black, (no blonde, they were upstairs), talking *on-and-on* about nothing. Saying the same thing *over-and-over-and-over* again.

About this time, another *aftershock* begins to hit the T.V. studios. The picture began to shake. I knew it was on its way. The seconds turning to hours and all…

And soon, it shook me too. No, not all night long, but enough to get my heart rate pumping up and going again.

It lasted for only a few seconds, but it began to make me realize a few things… There I was alone. No one had called. Why? I begin to think of who I should/could expect to call. And so, I went over to check my telephone phone line and except for an initial not immediate buzz, it seemed up and ready to go. But, the phone, it did not ring.

*   *   *

Alone, now alone sucks! Especially in moments of external crisis and all that. It is not bad; say when you are sitting in the late-night writing literature for the coming age. But alone.... It does not feel good.

Why hadn't my *Main L.A. Babe* called? Why hadn't my mother even called? I sat there listening to the prophets of doom on the T.V. repeat themselves, *over-and-*

over-and-over, while writing in my journal.

*   *   *

Speaking of my mother… Now, I guess, my mother has never been much of a mother. But then, it was not her who chose to have a son. So, I have been told. She was forty and massively career orientated; very selfish minded, and from the Midwest— *Uck.* My father, the L.A. kid that he was, wanted the child. So apparently, he blew his rocks one night, deep in their marriage, without telling my mother. He got his wish, such as it was.

Hell, my mother used to brag, *"All I did was smoke cigarettes and drink coffee when I was pregnant."* I have often wondered what my mind, my life, would have been like if I was not incubated in such a toxic environment.

And, she would often say, *"If I could have found an abortion, I would have gotten one."* They weren't legal back then…

And, therefore, and thereof, the other problem is/was, he, (my father), being the massive career orientated person that he was, as well, not only blew his rocks ten years the previous but blew his heart out in one massive *on-the-job* cardiac arrest, heart attack. So, there she was—my mother, and oh yes, me. My father, he was dead.

Now, this certainly isn't the first time something like this has happened in the annals of history. In some cases, the people step up to the challenge and raise a kid right. In other cases, (i.e. mine), my mother set about on a course that would destroy the mind and the psychological stability of even the *best-of-the-best;* while claiming she was doing it all for my own good. She was not.

She is an extremely selfish, vain, controlling person. In her time, she has destroyed a lot of lives, not just mine.

So, here I sit, walking a *fine-line* of existence; broken, yet functioning—though some would, no doubt, argue that fact.

But, as previously stated, this is not the first time this occurrence has occurred in the annals of history. Nor, will it be the last. Which guides us to the conclusion that life is a choice—you do with it what you will. You can take bad situations and do good things, or you can do the adverse. Doing good makes things better. Doing bad, makes things worse. And, the reality is; what you do/what you live all comes back to haunt you either in a positive or a negative manner.

In any case, we haven't spoken much lately; my mother and I. Basically, I am just sick of her attempts at manipulation and the intensive guilt she dishes out on all of my, *what she considers,* inadequacies in life. But, *none-the-less,* I thought it would have been nice for her to at least call. I don't even know where she is living now. So, I couldn't/can not call her.

*   *   *

As I sat there thinking—my mind wandered back to 1971. That was the last really big *e.g.* in L.A. How old was I? I must have been maybe twelve; maybe thirteen. I forget…

At the time, we; my mother and I, lived in this dump of a one-bedroom apartment in L.A., over on 6th Street. Well, the truth being told, it was a step up from the room in the old brick hotel we had inhabited and spent the previous year in on Normandie.

Now, the side note is… The note which needs to be mentioned; you see my mother always had money. My father and her were not rich, but were quite well off— being massively career orientated and all…

But, my mother, being a truly bread mid-westerner, *Uck,* of full-blood Scottish decent, and having lived through the *Great Depression,* always choose to live like a *nigger.* Now, I do not use that term in reference to race, but in reference to what society has deemed a *nigger:* low, poor, poor housing, poor area, poor environment, *etcetera.*

Like, you know, John Lennon sang, *"Woman is the Nigger of the World."*

I remember when that song was banned from all the radio stations. Back then, in about 1971... Which is what I am actually talking about here, not the other tangent.

I know, I know, a white guy, like myself, isn't suppose to use the term, *"Nigger,"* anymore. Even if it is in reference to a song like John Lennon's, *"Woman is the Nigger of the World,"* Or Patti Smith's, *"Rock n' Roll Nigger."* It comes off as racist, I guess. But, that is not where I'm coming from in this *re-ference.*

Fuck, man, you want to talk about racism... I remember when I the only Caucasian kid in my grammar school. Everyday of my life, when I wasn't getting jacked by five or six dudes at a time, I was being called, *"White Paddy,"* or *"Honky."* So, believe me, when I say, I know what racism is and/or is not.

Anyway, back to the story... We lived in this apartment and I was sleeping on the couch as I often did. The '71 *e.q.* came and me being young, fractured, and already on the way to being a psychological basket case, due to all the hell and abuse I had lived through in my youthful years. Well… I remember the shaking: the noise, the rumbling, the fear, the panic. I just got up and ran...

For a second—one of those seconds that last for an eternity; I was unable to find the bedroom. I ran into the bathroom. Remember, it was only a one-bedroom apartment. Finally, I found it, (the bedroom), and the only source of humanity I had any access to; my mother. Then, the eternity of the rumbling, the shaking, the panic ended.

That was then. My mother had to go to work that day—naturally… Being the massive career orientated person that she was. So she, at her usual 7:30 AM or so, bailed on out the door and to the bus stop— monthly bus pass in hand.

You see, we had a car, it is actually still in the families possession. A rather more than *bitchin' '66 Mustang,* that my father had purchased new before he died. The truth being told, however, he too was a horrible parent, though he did possess more than an ounce of style. But, the car, as with all our furniture—the furniture that wasn't given away, was shipped back to my mother's family home in a little *uck* place in Illinois. In fact, I too was shipped back to live with some relatives I barely knew a few days after my father's death.

That was on Christmas day, 1968. I was ten years old.

In fact, periodically, I was dumped back that direction, to be placed in the home of one of her relatives. Back and forth, three or four times, until I was about thirteen. Sent back to hell, while my mother would stay in funky old brick hotels and ride the dirty L.A. buses. *"I need the money,"* so she would tell the very distant hick cousins of hers prior to baling for the coast. This was of course all while she was sitting on several hundred thousand G's left from my father's business. …Him being massively career orientated and all.

Some people were just born to be *niggers,* even though they had white skin and dollars in the bank. You see, color has nothing to do with *nigger-dom.*

*   *   *

But, back to the story at hand… She went off to her high position in a small and growing company. Me, I was left alone as all *latch-key-kids* are.

Hey, I mean no big deal, you know, they even used to leave me home alone on all my school vacations when we lived in

Southcentral L.A. Then, my father was still alive. When I was four, five, six, seven, eight years old. *"Just be tough,"* they would say. But that—that was a long time ago.

But, back to '71...

The young dude, me, sat there alone, feeling all of the major *aftershocks.* The *aftershocks* of the morning, in the morning of the morning. The BIG ONE(s) always seem to happen in the morning.

What an alarm clock... I never have liked alarm clocks. Maybe that is why? But the AM gravitational pull and all seems to set off the *e.q's.*

Now, back then, 1971; my mother at work, my school closed for three days to check for any damage; I alone and seriously scared, as only alone little boys can be. Well, I called up my friend and headed over his direction, a few blocks away. Another kid left alone. His father, Cuban. Basically, a nice guy. They lived in a boardinghouse owned by an old white lady who drove a big old green Cadillac. He was poor; a trap of the world. Poor for no good reason. Poor for lack of the dollars. The trap of the infinite reality—the dollars.

I was there for a while, the boardinghouse place. We told each other how we handled it all. We spoke to the other people in the boardinghouse: a young guy, who had come out to L.A. and was going to art college, an older guy, had the boobs of a woman, said, *"Fuck,"* every other word, and a guy, middle-age, good temperament, if I knew how to express it than, *"One of those damn nice guys."* He was dying though, dying from stomach cancer.

We talked. We watched T.V. We felt the *aftershocks*. We were not alone. There were a group of us; old and young, alike.

Anything is better than being alone in times like that.

The time passed. It was still morning but acceptable morning, maybe 10:00 AM or so. I don't quite remember. But, I called my junior high school sweetheart. My first girlfriend. I called her on the pay phone in the boardinghouse of my friend. I called her and she invited me over. Invited me over to her house.

Her house, well it was more like a mansion, in the *Hancock Park* section of L.A. It had a pool, a tennis court, a basketball court, and all... *"All,"* is perhaps a good word to describe it.

And though, I could walk her home from school each day, *en route* to my abode, on the wrong side of the tracks, as it were. I could walk her home, but... I could never live up to her world. Not being one of those go for it all, *gold-digger* type of personalities. Her wealth and my living standard, the whole situation… Well, it did make me feel a bit uncomfortable.

She was beautiful though. A recent Manhattan Beach transplant with long blonde hair and granny glasses. She invited me, so I went. How could I say, *"No?"*

My friend, he was not alone. I would not have left, if leaving would have left him that way. He was in the arms of the others in the boardinghouse, who were also not alone.

I got on my *Schwinn* five-speed, *Apple Crate,* bicycle and off I went to the good side of town. There, the day passed, as the days do.

We, my girlfriend, and I; we talked for a while, listened to records for awhile in her room, and felt the *aftershocks* for awhile.

She even left me in the room of her brother/with her brother, for a very uncomfortable while. Why? I forget. But he had a T.V. in his room. We watched the reports, as we felt the *aftershocks.*

We said nothing, her brother and I. He didn't speak, not a word. I didn't speak. He lay in his bed. I stood leaning against the doorframe. A safe place, I guess…

I stood there wishing that she, my girl friend, would return.

He was a couple years older than I.

Back then, when a couple of years meant a lot. His hair was longer than mine. I remember how I noticed that. Things like that mattered back than in '71. But, my hair is probably longer than his is now—as most people grow up to be and become respectable citizens.

They all seem to live in a world where there is no room for that of the bohemian temperament. Most people, not me…

I went home that evening, after I was sure my mother had arrived. I rode my bike. Spoke to my boardinghouse friend on the telephone once I got home. He was AOK.

The next day was hard. I was alone. My mother had gone to work. My boardinghouse friend to his mother's place in Carson. I called, but my girl friend was, *"Out."* I was alone. I was scared.

I sat in the front doorway of our apartment looking out onto 6th Street. I had my red and white portable record player/radio next to me listening…

Listening to the bubble gum pop. Listening to the deejay who had been on the air, the day before, replay the tape of what had happened and how his record player needle slid across a monster hit.

Live radio. A long time ago.

I sat there staring off onto/into the inner city wasteland—alone. *Aftershock-to-*

aftershock, returning the fear to my mind.

My mother, being the maximum career orientated person that she was: at the job/on the job. Her world. My father's world too. *"The Job,"* I was alone.

I remember how for a year or three after that, the slightest shake; minor *e.q.,* would put *ultimate-fear* in my heart. I remember how years later, I heard a person speaking on an early morning radio talk show—some one calling in and asking the resident radio psychologist what they should do, for every time they felt a shaking, they had *the ultimate-fear.* She, the radio shrink, said it was a traumatic experience, 1971. *"It was/it is natural, don't worry."* So the shrink said… I remember how I thought, *"I was glad I was still not where the caller was in 1976, left at/in the ultimate-fear syndrome."*

I remember a few years after that, in my attorney's office, after I had become *Street Pizza,* had my skull/my face broken in numerous places. A bad motorcycle accident. Being introduced to the front right fender of a *Mercedes Benz,* turning left into me. Motored by an eighteen-year-old girl, who took me down like a slapped bitch. She claimed she didn't see me. My life/my body has never been the same.

I remember my attorney, Century City, twentieth floor, and all... He was speaking on the telephone, while I sat there, and he claimed he felt a shake to the other conversationist. He believed we had an *e.q.* I felt nothing. Turns out there was nothing, simply his *ultimate-fear.*

No control/No ability. Alone, nothing is left.

Enough of the foundational history. Back to the present...

Typical, my mother didn't call. She was obviously at work—involved/engulfed with the only thing that ever mattered to her; her high and powerful position in a once small company that had now become larger.

But, I could not help but wonder, *"Why hasn't my Main L.A. Babe called? Who else was there? Who else might call?"*

I searched my mind but there was no one else. No one else local, that is.

I mean, I go through babes like a whore in heat. I always leave *'em* heartbroken hearted, *hatein'* me. So, none of them are going to call...

Hell, I pretty much change my phone number ever couple of months, just to make sure that they don't... But, here/today; two people: my mother and my *Main L.A. Babe,* they should call. Now, my mother, well what can I say? But, my *Main L.A. Babe...* Well, her too, I guess. It's a long story...

But, in brief, just so you can catch the vibe; I have been more than *un-right* to her over the past six plus years that I have known her. So many times, I never wanted to see her again. And yet; by fate, destiny, virtue, karma, or pure foolishness, she has remained my only true female friend.

When I returned from my last, *Deep Asia Journey,* two months back, I swore to no longer associate with her. But, push comes to shove, and we have eaten out a lot, shopped a lot. And...

In all my life discontentment, I have even purchased her maximum dollars worth of gifts for her new apartment. Purchased, for my karmic salvation, for my foolishness, for my destiny, for my loneliness, for my desire to erase her pain. All this, and she didn't even call!

*   *   *

Mostly, it is very hard for me to come back from Asia. The big fish in a small pond syndrome. A place where *the all* and *the everything* is so fucking haveable/doable. Five Star hotels; the maid comes in each day. Just put the laundry by the door each morning. Room service, and internationally recognized chefs in the hotel restaurants. The other side/deep on the outside, places where no Caucasian men have ever travel before. And the babes... Just their availability... Man, it is the life. The life is there, not here—certainly not now. Not for me. Not on an L.A. *e.q.* day.

I remember my last, *Deep Asia Journey*. I rented a bike in Lhasa. I rode it for days deep into the outback of Tibet—seeking... All the children wanted was a picture of the *Dalai Lama.* I gave them all I had. I guess they were in search of life salvation too? I guess, I don't know?

*   *   *

But, back to here, to this AM. I attempted to be understanding. To tell myself perhaps her phone lines were down. Down; up there in the inner city, the *nuevo city,* Melrose Avenue, of the *laten-ing* 1980's.

She has always been selfish, though. She, my *Main L.A. Babe.* I guess that's what comes with beauty; comes with knowing you're beautiful. Come with, constantly being told you're beautiful.

She's a taker, by choice or by force. But me/today, I needed her. And, she was nowhere to be heard.

But, I am no fool. I realized/all I could think was, *"God, she needed me so many times and where was I? Romancing some other woman in some distant, far off land. So, I guess, this is just karma."*

*   *   *

Oh, and by the way… Now, you see, in most instances, one could just telephone a person up. Like hey, I could have called her… But no, she won't give me her telephone number.

"Why," you ask?

You see, she doesn't want me to call her in the late night; the Bohemian night— my night. The time when she and I lived our relationship to the fullest. The time when she and I used to thrive. We would go out and eat late-night apple pie with melted cheese upon it, *alamode,* at *Denny's,* and drink the java deep. Eat chili cheeseburgers at *Tommy's* off Alvarado. Go to the *twenty-four-seven* newsstand on Cahuenga, in Hollywood. Take long walks on *The Strand,* or on the South Bay Piers. Hell, sometimes; back then—back when we were young/back when we were in love, we would have sex, after sex, after sex. There was a lot of things that we did back then. Back then. Not now.

Food/activities/and the time zone made only for the dreamer(s). Those who chose to live outside the norm. Those who desire to dance the dance of destiny. But now, she has moved into the peripheries of the mainstream. You see she works nine-to-five at the *L.A. County Museum of Art.* She sells tickets. Arty, I guess? But, *nine-to-five, none-the-less.*

*   *   *

It is always so sad, I think, how modern society, *"The World,"* if you will, soaks up all the style, all the art, and forces it into the nothingness of nine-to-five—solely for/as a means of existence. So few have any vision at all. Fewer still can fight away the wages of, *"The World."*

But, let me lay a side note on you here. Since I am speaking about the speaking of…

A funny/interesting little *thAng…*

Anyway, as mentioned, she works for LACMA. She sells tickets at the window. The passageway to the realms of art. Art; the source point for illusion.

In any case, she got *talkin'* to a coworker of hers—a guy. They got talking about love, lust, art, god, and whatever… She mentions me. He knows me. *"We went to high school together,"* he exclaims. *"He was such a positive influence to me. He was such an inspiration. Whenever I had a problem, I would talk to him (me). He was so spiritual."*

When I heard this story, all I could say was, *"Wow."* Sure, I remembered the dude. A friend kinda… I guess…

In tenth grade, *Hollywood High School,* we hung/we got high. But me, I always felt like an outsider in that/his crew.

They, his group, had all grown up together. Me, I had moved in from *The Hood.*

They all lived in big houses up in the Hollywood Hills. Me, I lived in a furnished apartment on the wrong side of the tracks.

But, where you live, doesn't define your spirituality, I guess. In fact, all the violence I lived through, up until that point in my life; you know, in *The Hood.* Well, it probably helped to shape my, *"Spiritual,"* mindset. And, I, of course, use the word, *"Spiritual,"* quite loosely.

But yeah, I guess I was/I am/can be seen as a, *Spiritual Being.* If you want to call it that… But, terms like, *"Spiritual," "Religious,"* I don't know, they kind of weird me out. I don't think they do a good job of defining what, *"Spirituality,"* is actually about.

But, back then, back in high school, I used to speak of the *Tao Te Ching, Yoga, Zen,* and the like. In fact, I left the world of drugs and that crew, (that guy's crew), to pursue what I had to pursue on the spiritual side of the photograph.

But, it just struck me as so strange, how anyone would/could remember me so vividly and call me an influence. From then, way back then... I've gotten that a lot since then. But, then... Back then... *Strange...*

So, that's the back-story.

One day I went by the museum. The girl, my *Main L.A. Babe;* well, she had set up a meet. The dude, him and me. Good enough to see him. Nothing really to say. The years, they had piled on.

But, it struck/strikes me as so strange that even then, people were listening to what I had to say. Listening, and I didn't even know it. Who's the fool? Them or me? I do not know?

*   *   *

But, back to this story... The one at hand—the *e.q.* and all.

Where did I leave off? Oh yeah, my *Main L.A. Babe.*

Anyway, she also doesn't want me to call her in the 5:00 AM hours of the, *stay-*

up-all-night, morning either—to go and have a special chili omelet or the like at *The Kettle* in Manhattan Beach. The facts being told, the only reason I know where she lives at all, is that I purchased her a drafting table which she desired a month or so ago. And, in her having no way to get it home, I was instrumental in the task.

Instrumental and an instrumentalist.

*　　*　　*

I flipped through the T.V. stations. I found another news channel which was more appealing. It had facts, not fiction. And though redundancy played a part in its presentation, as well, *"For all those who have just tuned in. . . "* you know, it was better on the whole than the previous station.

There was an Asian lady at the helm. It made me remember how today, Thursday, was to be the day, the contact point of new love in the third degree. I have/had been visualizing/crystallizing/materializing, and have heard the inner voice, *"Today's-the-day. New love in the third degree."*

Minus the *e.q.,* I had planned to do my traditional Thursday *thAng; Farmer's Market* on 3rd and Fairfax session. You know, go have a *cafe au lait* and read the

L.A. Weekly, 2:30 P.M. ish. My tradition… And there/then to meet the new.

Actually, I had not been at my traditional Thursday session for the last few weeks due to my *Main L.A. Babe*'s Thursday day off schedule. She always wanted to hang…

Today was going to be different! When she called, as it was Thursday, I knew that she would, I was going to tell her,

"Look, I have been answering all of your needs; when you need something/want something, I get it for you, (the world of plastic passion, until it takes itself to the limit, and all). But you, you have not been answering any of my needs. I have been a friend to you. But, you have not been one to me."

I was going to tell her that. But....

The *e.q.* came this morning. It shook. And… A second of aloneness turns into its own eternity of *on-trial-ness;* in the jury and judgment of pagan reality—that of aloneness.

Lost in the sunshine of a wall of silence that has no perfection, no essence; only the all that is, in it's own nothingness.

*   *   *

One of the, *Special Report,* news teams then began to address, *"All of you who are alone. . ."*

I sat there, just over there on Mr. Couch, and realized, I am not even thirty years old, not yet, and I am so fucking alone. I know it is/was me who had made it that way. I Orchestrated my own destiny, as we all do. But...

The statement made me remember back to a movie I saw of this guy up in the mountains and the snow almost trapped him in his cabin and when he finally got out, he was screaming, *"I am so alone."* There I was, this morning, *"So alone!"*

Now, I have a friend or three. But, the kind of *hard-guys* I hang with you just don't call unless you're dead, dying, in jail, have your mind on getting seriously fucked up in the drink *departmento,* or have two or more babes on the line that have guaranteed pussy to pass out.

And, for all the rest of my people that go back to the day; the *more-or-less* normal ones—married and what have you... Well, they have their own lives and their own personal melodramas. Oh, I mean involvements.

And women, well, as mentioned, (and for anyone who knows me), there have been more than a few which I could/should have hung onto to, shacked up with, hell, even married… In fact, there was even a passing/fleeting moments I thought to marry this one, my *Main L.A. Babe,* when I was cribbed up in Shanghai a few months back and had gotten a little disillusioned/or delusional, (depending on how you want to look at it), with the Asian flavoring… But that's a different novel. But they/it/them/the situation(s), never seemed to answer my needs or my overall desires.

What does all this equal? Alone.

Okay, all this nonsense being adequately stated… I resolved as I sat here alone this AM—is morning, to never to be so alone again. Again, as the fourth *aftershock* stirred my panic consciousness.

*   *   *

The newscast talked *on-and-on-and on.* I lay on Mr. Couch watching it/listening to it; appreciating the beauty of this mid-forties Asian newscaster; noting, that one of the in-the-field-reporter's hair was long dark brown, flowing, and beautiful. She looked an amazing amount like that of my *Main L.A. Babe*, who still hadn't called!

Where was she? Was she alright? Was her phone not working? Or, was she just the same way, the way she has become: selfish, unthinking, self-centered? It wasn't always that way...

There was a time: four, five, six years ago—before I fucked around on her three hundred times—let her catch me more than once. Before I insulted her; pushing her buttons of deep psychological pain, and abused her. Yeah, there was a time that she actually cared/actually loved me the best. But, that was a long time ago. And, I fucked it up *big-time*. *Big-time* and perhaps the saddest news is that I didn't even care. Not then/not now.

We all dig our own graves. The sad thing about it all is, however, that the *Heaven or Hell* we are taught/we experience as children is really what influences us—causes us to act, and makes us who we are. *We can never escape our childhoods.*

That being said, we all choose our own paths: be it acceptance or rebellion; based in what we have encountered. Somehow, in all the truth of choice, all the truth of perfection, and all the lies of religion, there is influence and environment. What and why, creating our minds before we are ever clear about anything. Somehow, it all creates us as we create it. Somehow. . .

As the television broadcast continued, speaking of the buildings that had collapsed, the parking structure that went down at a university, (CSULA), which I once attended for graduate school. It went down/fell down, crushing a lady.

I remember I had sex in the back of my bad little VW pickup truck in that parking structure once upon a time, along time ago. Oh, just for the record, it did have a camper shell on it and it was carpeted.

Yeah, she was this chick on the *so-so* side of the picture; a touch on the chubby side. Korean flavor. Had come here on a student visa. Was in a grad class with me.

Claimed she was a virgin. She was not—at least she wasn't anymore... But, like all passing fantasies, it was just a do it cause it was there and available sort of *thAng*.

Sad, I guess, I don't even remember her name.

*   *   *

The newscaster spoke of those who had died of heart attacks, (not being able to control the boundaries of life can lead to the big H.A.). She spoke of the people trapped in downtown elevators. Of all those on the streets afraid to go inside/go home;

conversing, relieving their stress. *"A good medicine,"* as the reporter put it. And though I too wished to converse, to not be alone, there was no one.

Then, I felt sleepy. It was hard for me to believe but there I was lying on Mr. Couch totally having no control of what may or may not happen next to Mother Earth. Yet, I was tired.

It was now maybe 9:30 AM or so. The point of perfection hit. I turned off the T.V., rolled over, and went back to sleep; expecting an *aftershock* would probably wake me up anyway. And me, with nothing left to lose. . .

I slept. I dreamt. The dream was that I found a new place to live. It seemed to be close to *Little Tokyo.* The structure/the building, in the dream, it had a big sign saying, *"Lhasa."* I felt so happy. I had found a community touched by Tibet. *My Tibet Journey '87.* Yeah, it was quite an adventure.

As I sit here now, typing these words onto the keyboard of my computer, I look up and see a Tibetan *thanka* of *the Goddess.* I purchased this *thanka* deep in outback regions of Tibet a few months ago.

Ah, *the Goddess,* what an effect/affect she has had upon my life; luring me, as is her part in the scheme of this universe; how she has brought me joys and at times, (more than a few), hung me out to dry. Ah, *the Goddess*... It all makes me reaffirm my desire to return to her land, her realm—Asia.

Lhasa, my dream. *Lhasa* in my dreams. I was surrounded by Tibetan monks, Tibetan children: dancing, playing. I walked up to a Tibetan prayer wheel, which I saw, and spun it three times. Just then, the telephone rang. It the real world. Not in my dream.

The telephone rang; it awoke me from my Tibetan dream. I looked at the clock as I moved towards the ringing telephone. It was 11:08 AM.

There had been no more noticeable *aftershocks.* At least none strong enough to wake me. But it was 11:08 AM and she had called. She, my *Main L.A. Babe.*

I could hear from the background noises that she was not at home. I inquired as to her whereabouts. She was out shopping. I told her of my feelings about her and our relationship. You know, the words I mentioned a few lines back.

What I did not mention, (a few lines back), was that the whole reason I played this *Mr. Nice Guy* game with her was that it was my way of delving down deep into my heartless or soulless being, (depending on how you play the card), and trying to find a bit of remaining humanity. Was there any left? I don't know? I doubt it… But, *none-the-less,* I tried to find some. I tried to play nice. Nice… To try and make up for all the years of *un-right* I had dished her. There is no doubt that I was/am an asshole to that beautiful girl.

Did it work/Could it work? I doubt it. But, I tried, *none-the-less…*

On the other end of the telephone line she told me the reason she didn't call earlier was because she knew that I didn't like to wake up before eleven in the AM.

Okay, I buy that…

Then, *re: my discussion about how I felt she was behaving incorrectly,* she told me if I was, *"Icky,"* then she wouldn't come over.

"Icky," I smiled… I chilled.

Amazement of all amazements, she was actually going to drive over. Since she has moved from the South Bay, it has been I who has been doing the predominance of all the driving up to the mid-to-late 1980's *nuevo hip* Melrose.

I generally pick her up at the newsstand off of Fairfax, so her roommate-sister won't tell her nosey mother that I am still around and hanging tough/hanging tight. Sometimes, when I am allowed to and when no one is looking, I am given permission to drive in front of the temple, her apartment, and she comes out.

Now, she used to spend some time driving over to see me. As we haven't officially lived together in years. My choice (by the way). But, amazingly, she was going to drive over today. Come down to the beach.

I mean, I told you of my plans for the day. But with the *e.q.* and all I had decided not to go to *Farmer's Market* today, anyway. Due to the traffic, the people, the lack of control, and all…

So, after having said my piece to her, I resolved myself to spend the day, eat some breakfast, and exist in the state of not being alone, with her. Her, my *Main L.A. Babe*.

With her *en route,* I put a few things away. The kind of things it would be better if she did not see. You know, leftover other chick items… I do have a bit of a collect of bras and panties building up by the side of my bed. *Hey, we all need to collect something don't we?*

I put them away and then I waited… As I waited, I watched the continuing saga of the *e.q's Special Bulletin* newscast(s) and remained incomplete in my dressing attire. This was due to the fact that she, my *Main L.A. Babe*, often times becomes angered if I am dressed in a way she does not deem appropriate. This generally means, she thinks I am too dressed up for what she is wearing.

The basic joke is, I always wear pretty much the same thing everyday: baggy, generally cuffed pants, a shirt buttoned to the top button, untucked, of course, a sport coat, and tennis shoes. Now, if this always be the case, as it always is, it is logical that it is simply a color or a fabric make-up that would infuriate her.

Life and its eccentrics and neurotics. And when, like I, one falls into both categories. Her too...

*   *   *

She arrived, what I considered a bit late. But, fashionable late and all... And, oh yes, she is beautifully fashionable.

I was given clear reign on what I could wear. She wasn't going to check into the insane asylum of insecurity this day. Thank god...

I choose a favorite pair of very baggy green pants and a paisley white/blue shirt. Both of which made the journey to Tibet with me, (as detailed, a couple of months the previous). I grabbed a gray, extra large, double-breasted, cool lapelled, sport coat.

For the record, lapel styling is what really makes or breaks a sport coat.

I finished off my outfit with my *New Balance 1300s,* (Philippines, Thailand, and Japan), traveled tennis shoes. The basics of which I am wearing now.

Though I had wanted to go to this little Belgium Waffle place that we frequent in San Pedro's, *Ports-O-Call,* my *Main L.A. Babe* didn't want to climb on board the sugar express. Being the understanding and more than nice guy I had momentarily become, I agreed, avoided the fight, and we went local and had a quiche.

We could have chilled each others bones over who was going to drive but, aside from the basic, *"You drive!" "No, you drive,"* joke or two, and all the excuses thereof, we just got into my bad little '64 *Porsche 356 SC.* And, we were off.

Over brunch, we discussed the *e.q.* as the whole restaurant was alive with words of the same. We spoke of 1971. She, that day, got braces put on. She remembered it well. Her school was not closed, as was mine. For her family had moved from Southcentral to Hawthorne—which was way far from the epicenter. So she—she went in to school late. Her classmates all thought her fearful of the shaking and quaking, as the reason for her tardiness. But, once she opened her mouth, their misunderstandings were corrected.

For the record and to cast reality to the sands of time, she has a family, a safety net; not too large not too small. Each of her family members neurotic and/or way fucked up in their own way, just like her. Though she probably would/will be angered in my saying that. But, this world is so full of neurosis; so much abnormality. What is normal? Certainly not those who think that all is clear-cut. That life is simply *nine-to-five,* family, and die. They are the fools and in for a seriously rude awakening. But, blood is thicker than water, so the saying goes. A family usually means, *"Not alone."*

I have no family. Thus, I am alone.

I told her of my 1971 experience and the aloneness I felt today. She told me I was dwelling on my own misery. Maybe she was/is right.

One does not have to like life to accept life. Acceptance leads to freedom. Acceptance means not seeking control. Not seeking control, means no death from heart attacks when there is an e.q.

So we ate, drank some java, and within and without a need for any accomplishment, we drove onto the day/our day.

As the temperatures across the city begin to rise, we moved into the well-known world—well known to her and I—shopping and the shopping center.

Our first stop was a bike shop. I needed to pick up some new handle bar tape for my *Colnago.*

I had spent a rather frustrating yesterday doing a major *clean-it-up* and overhaul on it. Those several hours combined with adjustment(s) on my ATB proved disconcerting.

My new apartment, though beautiful in location and view, leaves much to be desired in the form of space and usability. For an artist, poet, musician, photographer, bike rider, and general dreamer like myself, space is of premium importance. Yet, having grown up in the hell(s) of this city: Southcentral and East Hollywood, with a stint in general L.A., (now they call it *Koreatown),* I just do not wish to dwell in say the *Loft District* of Downtown and pay two dollars a square foot and have the very probable chance of having the loft building be my burial tomb on an *e.q.* day in L.A. such as today. As actually took place for some very unsuspecting tenants this day. I saw it on the *Special Report.*

*   *   *

The bike shop was uneventful. I got the handlebar tape. An employee overtly checked out my *Main L.A. Babe.* I laughed to myself. *"You can have her,"* I thought. *"If he only knew..."*

The owner gave me the main and basic, *"Hello. How you doing?"* How he even remembers me; I don't know. Even though I did buy a couple of Italian bike frames from him, a year past.

Once queried upon the said topic, as we walked outside, my *Main L.A. Babe* tells me it is due to the, *"Look,"* I have.

"And so, everyone remembers you," she says.
I tell her, *"Yeah, but it makes me nervous."*
She replies, *"Then don't have long hair, earrings, and wear stylish, expensive clothing."*

Simple truths, spoken to all the insecure, low self-esteem people, usually based in the psychology lack of acceptance during their childhood, like me. *"Word,"* to all those individuals, *Break'n Fly,* looking for acceptance and love in the arms of strangers. Me, I'm with you. . .

Along with my telling her how the guy was checking her out, which she didn't believe. She never does...

You see, she has a problem with realizing how stunningly beautiful she really is, though everybody keeps *tellin'* her. Long, wavy brown hair, Spanish eyes, and radiant style.

But, ego stroked as ego goes. I got to mentioning my very special *Colnago Equilateral* bike frame in the presence of a customer. You could see the envy in his eyes. My babe and my bike. *Ego: a fool's elixir; a mystic's poison.*

We then cruised on over to a house-wares store; where she, my *Main L.A. Babe,* spent about *forty-five* searching the walls, studying the sheets, the comforters, and the lining paper for drawers—which she claimed she so immediately needed. Me. Well... I began to notice something coming over me: the gift of God for the day/of the day.

Somehow the time, it just didn't seem to matter. Did not matter, as it usually does. There was no place to rush to, no place to rush away from. No journey to dream of. No journey to make.

You know, it is like, normally, I would count the hours, watch the moments pass on days like this. Somewhere else more

50

important to be. Something to see. Do, needed doing.

But today, it was all gone. *Zero.*

I did not have to watch the time for traffic, for I was not far from home. I did not have to sit and lament—bemoan of being alone. For I was with someone. I did not even feel the intensity of the, *"I have to get home to create,"* pressures. Which I have the tendency to feel—in a seemingly no pressure, artist's, world.

Pressure lurks in the strangest guises.

I was away, doing away with it all. Doing it all, as nothing was not being done. Sounds almost like something written in some translation of the, *Tao Te Ching.* But, being nowhere, seemed like being everywhere.

From there, we headed over to the main scene, where no man can ever come out alive. The flamboyant video, in the colors of neon; *The Shopping Mall.* And though I had purchased her, my *Main L.A. Babe*, an outfit or three the evening last, at *The Beverly Center,* she claimed, as the mall's structure came into view, (just about twelve hours ago as I now study the digital timepiece which sits on my apartment's bar, over there/over my shoulder), that I had not taken her to this particular *Shopping Mall* in a very long time. Like that was some sort of a sin.

Anyway, we played the typical W.T. (White Trash), go to *The Shopping Mall* game, *"Let's see how closely we can park, so we don't have to waste any of our energy walking three extra feet to the door, so we can save it, (the energy that is), to walk around The Shopping Mall a million times."*

I got in close—real close. Two parking spaces from the door—the main door. She was happy about this fact. She, my *Main L.A. Babe.*

I was clean. My *Porsche* was dirty. All of us, wearing the disguise of W.T.

Into *The Shopping Mall* we went. Into a department store, a major department store, we landed. We looked at the jewelry counter, as she decided upon the perfect version, of the perfect model, of this one perfect piece; being the perfectionist of a purchaser that she is. A perfect purchase, we eventually forgot to make. We were going to pick it up on our way out.

I was later blamed as to our forgetfulness. *Me being blamed, of course...*

I strolled over to the suit section, in this major department store, and looked at the lapels. I tried one on. Nothing too exciting—nothing too baggy.

We made our way out into the main corridor and promenaded in all of our style. She wore this long, semi tight, black skirt with a slit up the back; just the way she likes *'em,* just as is her style; combined with: a black sweater and a pair of men's *wing tips* covering her white socks. She does have style.

As for me, I already told you what I was *a-style'n* in. *Lookin' FLY.*

We chilled at a place or thirty. The shopping, the day, was hers. We put in a quick appearance at this Italian clothing shop, I generally like, and found massive amounts of just under $100.00 kill shirts and some mega *bitchin'* pants. The sport coats were, in my appraisal, none too happening, however. The lapel cut just didn't make it.

I fought my way out of the walls of the store. My credit cards still intact in my two wallets. Yes, it's true. I carry two; count *'em,* two wallets.

I made it out. Though I may have to return tomorrow.

*   *   *

A side note here... While there, yes there was a guy working the floor. Probably Armenian, as that is the crew that owns this store. Maybe Italian... In any case, a good *lookin'* dude, at least in the eyes of my woman. She liked what she saw: dark hair, dark eyes, greased back ponytail, and clothing supplied by said location. She smiled my directed, letting me know her mind. Seeing if I was jealous. Internally, I laughed. For as pretty as she is; my *Main L.A. Babe,* she doesn't understand that any girl can get fucked, all they have to do is put themselves up on the chopping block and there will be a million dudes willing to take a try. But, love; the love she desired; well, that is a different creature, a different animal.

I smiled back. Gave her the, *"Go for it"* nod. She did not.

End, side note...

*   *   *

We continued on, and through my focusing and ever-increasing relationship with my *Spirit Helper,* I materialized some very beautiful paper that would be perfect to line her drawers. Which was, in fact, on sale for only $4.00

It was actually in a very unique clothing store which we came to pass. And, as to whether or not it was supplied by my *Spirit Helper* to aid me in keeping from purchasing her, my *Main L.A. Babe*, very expensive drawer paper, (as I continually end up buying her what she wants), or whether it was simply placed in my field of reference to be cast to literature for the spiritually seeking masses, I do not yet know. *None-the-less,* it all was put into place. She got her desired object. I stayed within the realm of my monetary allotments. She could now place beautiful drawer paper in the antique chest which I purchased for her new apartment, two days ago.

*   *   *

Have you ever been in contact with your *Spirit Helper?* Have you ever visualized and had the desire you desired come to you? Think about it?

Perhaps I could best describe it, *the projection of desire into reality,* by telling you a tale of Thailand.

It was maybe a year or so ago. I had fallen in love, as I tend to do, with the lying daydream of a Thai girl. However, that is all a different story in another book. Anyway, I had really desired to find her a copy of the *Tao Te Ching.* No doubt, the most pure of all formalized spiritual writings. We had gone to this bookstore, in a newborn, ten story *Shopping Mall.* I had been there before. I looked throughout the metaphysical section of the store for the text. It was not to be found. I checked all other possible subject locations. But, nothing. It was very important I give this girl the *Tao Te Ching*, however. So, I went back to the metaphysical section. I very consciously and sincerely looked again. It was not there. I begin to focus my energy very precisely. A few moments past. In no uncertain terms, my eyes glanced and several copies of it were upon a shelf. Call it what you like. I know, through past and post experience(s), what I believe it to be. Now, if I could just find a way to do that with money, many of my problems would be solved.

*   *   *

We, my *Main L.A. Babe* and I, finally made our way to a more than interesting, stylishly shop for women. I mean, *it was like all the rage.* Inside, not only did she, my *Main L.A. Babe,* find two more than beautiful outfits to try on. But I, me, well there was this more than interesting Asian babe working the floor. She had on blue pant and red shoes.

Why is it that *style'n* Asian babes always wear red shoes? Like hey, *The Angels Want to Wear My Red Shoes.*

And, she wore a sweater that exposed the fact that she did have some seriously nice boobs. Perhaps, what was even more unique about her was the fact that she had this beautiful, *do.*

Now, many Asian women have the basic modern, trendy bowl cut. You know, a little longer on one side than the other. But hers, she had one side extremely long.

For that type of hair and that type of *style'n* chick, *sproutin'* that type of *style'n* cut; I mean she looked *kill to the max.*

My *Main L.A. Babe* kept giving me the raised eyebrows, *"Go for it."* look. She, my *Main L.A. Babe,* understanding my current preoccupation and desire for love, lust, and everything in between—well, she wanted me to make my move.

Now, this may be a surface exhibition on her part, of course. For in the past, she has been *big-time* jealous. She currently is in the mode of simply being friends. Which is AOK with me.

As she is riding close to the edge of sheer insanity. Chosen, of course, by herself. As we all make all our own choices, you know. But, her way of staying sane it to not love me to the max like she has done for the past six years. As mentions, I have done her wrong way too many times…

In-any-case and *none-the-less,* she wants to keep me around, to keep her grounded. I don't know if I can do that: stay around or ground her; either/or.

But anyway, she tried the clothing on. I hung nonchalant, just incase there was some love in the works with me and the chick *workin'* the floor. I gave the basic psychic love connection; you know, put a thought in the mind of the reflection of the Asian girl with the *do* which I saw in the mirror. But then, I realized, that I would never have good feelings about it if the babe didn't come my direction on her own.

*   *   *

in the chaotic embrace of passion
the reluctant love of mind
a look/a glance
into the eyes of particular beauty
ecstasy in its own proportions
giving a cry
for the embrace of love

for only if there were
or if there could be
the space
where attraction finds attraction
and all that we want
we can have

but when all that there is
is all that you want
there never seems to be enough room

mind in play
how it loves to dance
wanting/needing
is there a difference

you can feed the hungry
but sooner or later
they too will die

a desire embraced in the arms of passion
has no where to go
but on to another dream

in a world
my world
where any dream will do

*   *   *

As I caught my reflection in the mirror, I realized that it was true, what she, my *Main L.A. Babe*, had been saying, *"I was thin. Too skinny. I looked like a junky."*

I had dropped a lot of weight on the last deep Asia journey. And, upon returning to *the States,* seeing no reason to put it back on, haven't.

My face looked thin. My body felt thin. I felt good light; more muscular than I have ever been. Yet, there was something missing in my external appearance. Something. . .

Out of the dressing room she came. And though, the salesgirl, shoulder pads in hand, worked on the outfit, the clothing didn't do much for her. Her, my *Main L.A. Babe.* I studied the sales-chick's *do* closer, and realized as nice as it was, it had been cut very poorly. She needed a new *do* stylist.

"I'll think about it," she, my *Main L.A. Babe,* told the girl.

We leave. We walked out, into the masses on an *e.q.* day in L.A. We headed, as per her, my *Main L.A. Babes* suggestion, over to this *cappuccino inner-mall/inner-place,* where we poured *dos* down.

As we toasted the java's, my *Main L.A. Babe,* having been very aware of the location of my eye-line inside the clothing store, stated,

"You should go back into the store and pick up."

I told her, *"The chick obviously thought you were my girl friend."*

"Maybe not, I could just be your friend. We can go back in and make a comment to that effect."

"People aren't like clothing," I countered. *"Just because you like a look doesn't mean you can just go in and buy them."*

"You'd be surprised," she answered. *"And, I saw her checking you out."*

"I didn't notice that."

"I saw that smile she gave you when she was getting that sweater down for me."

"Where was I? I didn't see it."

"She did."

"Maybe the other girl, the one behind the register... Now, I noticed her checking me out."

"No, the Asian one was too. She's just your flavor."

It went back and forth for awhile. Nothing was solved, gain, contained, or refrained. I was still sitting there, locked in my brain, believing that, *"Any dream will do."* She was still there; her, my Main *L.A. Babe*, saying to, *"Go for it."*

She suggest going back in and she would say how,

"My friend thinks that you are very beautiful."

But me, I, being the keep the peace kind of guy that I am said,

"I only think that she is so-so beautiful."
"But, that's okay." she insisted.
"But, she's not perfect poetry like you."

I express this final statement, of course, in all of my purest form of male bullshit. You know, chicks always talk the talk, but inside their hearts are breaking. I didn't want to break her heart any further than I already had. ...Had, in times gone past.

It came down, as we finished up the last drops of our very bitter, too much foam, *cappuccino,* that she didn't want to go back in alone to set me up with another girl. And, I could find no dynamic motivation to make myself look like a total macho jerk, with the very decided possibility of mega rejection, to go in there; into a woman's shop, clothing store to pick-up; as chic as it may be.

The view outside was nice though. Out, through a window to my right.

Smog covered the city on this, an L.A. *e.q.* day. I sat there for a moment, studying the shapes, the forms of the city. I could see downtown, downtown L.A., from our perch and seat on the fourth floor facing strategically in that direction.

Downtown and the city. If I looked very hard and squinted a bit, I even could make out the Hollywood sign.

L.A. and the Hollywood sign, I spent my High School days growing up beneath it. Ah life, and the movements of ultimate nothingness within this city. This city on an L.A. *e.q.* day.

There was the 405 freeway down below—moving in all its flowingness. Movement, identical to the earth moving. But movement, it is all the same; to nowhere, going nowhere, for no energy can be created or destroyed; just moved around a bit. Just like life.

"So what shall we do," I questioned.
"I don't know, what do you want to do," she returns.
"Well, we can go to my place and snort some coke. I have a couple of grams laying around."
"You haven't done any of that yet?"
"No. See, that shows you I'm not addicted."
"That's what all the drug addicts and alcoholics say," she exclaims.

"Funny," I thought to myself, how I had been sitting on these couple of grams of

the toot for over a month now. Any other fool would have done them down. But me, I, never was one for *gettin'* fucked up alone. Though I have, in fact, done so, once or three hundred times. I actually hadn't done any coke for more than a month, since my *L.A. Party Bud,* Saturday Jim, and I did an all-nighter; shooting down four grams, along with wetting our lips to the extreme; while *sittin'* in his living room. All this, while his wife and his child slept soundly/calmly, never knowing a thing.

His wife doesn't let him do that kind of stuff anymore, you see. Even though, a few years back, her nose used to be sufficiently powdered, as well. But, anyway...

Basically, I had been sitting on the coke waiting for a new dream to come along. Where was she?

*   *   *

I, engulfed in my thoughts, sat there; location same, thinking/spacing out how, here I was again offering her, my *Main L.A. Babe*, my money, my illusion of waiting for a dream, and the resources thereof. Funny how we all get caught it our own prescribed prisons.

Wack! I get an *under-the-table* kick in the shin.

"What are you thinking about?"
"Nothing just spacing."
"Lets go," she exclaimed.

As we moved from table onto continued folly, we exited the *cappuccino* stand located with the walls of a rather pricey, major department store, and instantaneously her eyes came upon a beautiful long brown skirt with a top to match. Now, brown had been her sought after desire for the past week or so. It, brown clothing, appeared and had continued to do so. They just hadn't been the, *"Right one,"* yet.

A projection of her desire? A conscious projection of my desire to make her happy? Purchase her suffering from her, so it may be cast into the shadows of the fires of *Angi*.

Ever realize how much of this world is your own projection? How much control you actually have over it all—if you simply choose to develop it/exercise it? As the ancient yogis taught, *"The only one that exists in this world is you."*

She tried it on. It was all-right. Complete with the little slit up the back of the skirt, depictive of her unique style. It was about $100.00 or so and it was rung up and charged in my typical plastic passion manner by this young little beauty girl of Latin origin, who was obviously digging my scene. Probably just wanted some dude who would spend change like this on her. . .

We exited the store only to return a few minutes later to pick up a bracelet that she, my *Main L.A. Babe*, had seen and decide was, *"Hers."* The same sweet, late teens, young Latin *thAng,* rang my platinum plastic passion up again.

As we waltzed out, I was told,

"See all the babes like you. You saw how she was checking you out, didn't you?"
"They don't like me, they just think I'm eccentric and they can't figure me out."
"No way, they want it! Come on, you never had a problem getting women when you were lying and telling me we were forever."
"It was all different before. I was younger. I had more contact with people. I mean, what do I have to offer a woman? I'm a total flake."
"You're beautiful."

"But, I can't commit."
"So what! Women don't figure that out for a long time. Look how long it me. They just want a fine fashion accessory like you to walk them around."
"Come on, you know this city, chicks all want a steady man, with a steady job. Not a dreamer, a mystic, with nothing better to do than go shopping like me."

The conversation was going nowhere and after I made my final decline to head back into the chic shop, with the babe and the *do,* we decided to exit, stage left.

We left *The Shopping Mall;* got into my officially W.T. located and parked *Porsche* and sat back for a few. Both of us realizing that this day; it had a weird feeling.

* * *

Somehow the heat on this autumn *e.q.* day—somehow it moved the feelings into a weird space. The colors of the day; the sunlight, they all seemed orange—a strange orange.

I thought for a moment that it might be my prescription sunglasses. Sliding them slightly down my noise, I looked over the top of 'em. But no, it was the day. It was not my glasses. It was orangeish; orangeish gray. Colored by the smog. Colored from the feeling, from the wonder of when the next *aftershock* may occur. When will it occur?

As I write now, 3:48 AM, another noticeable *aftershock* has not yet hit. Nothing in the physical/material/earth sense of the word. But, that is not the case for the slight variations in my feelings, in my knowledge of the feelings, of what can/could/would occur.

*   *   *

But we, my *Main L.A. Babe* and I, mostly, we sat in my car deciding where to g0—where to shop next. Something I, something she, does oh so well.

But then, it came to me… I embraced it.

There I was in the car: in the heat, living on an L.A. *e.q.* day. I had no desire for this or for that. There was nowhere to be. I was not doing. I simply was being. And, my not doing, it just was.

This is/was a feeling which I have known sometimes. Sometimes, not lately; the mixtures of the world and all.

It was at that moment, like a flash of *Nirvana,* I knew. I knew to write this, *"e.q."*

Being/doing, *"Where do you want to go now?"* She named the stake. I started the car and we moved on.

* * *

a look in the field of vision
hazy orange and gray
the movement as no movement is
the placement
in the abstraction of the feeling
the knowledge
of the whisper faintly heard
of desire for the feeling
desire for the choice
a choice
in no choice
be it as it may

the feel of vision
abstract realities
in a expressionistic day
where the heat
is just a degree too high
heat on an Autumn day
where the feeling of anxiety
rides its way
non-stop into the soul
caring for nothing
killing all in its path
in a world

in a space
where there is no control

this day
it felt weird
as its orange and grayness
stood in the sunlight sky
making it
just a degree too warm
a feeling too uncontrollable
and a knowledge too deep
there was nothing

*   *   *

We moved on down the boulevard to the next place deemed worthy on her, my *Main L.A. Babe's,* shopping agenda. People with an agendas… I don't know. It never was me.

She, though; she had a place to be. It was this cool little import store.

Parked; then inside. She, checked out this rod-iron kitchen *thAng*. You know, the thing you use to hang pots and pans from. I went to study the Goddess—the statues her. The reminders of the journeys not so long ago and not so far away.

I picked up the iconic images, felt each of their appropriate given energies and feelings.

How I love the Goddess, though she has taken me for a ride or thirty. My believing, my love, my lost lust.

The Goddess, the base of all illusion. She is such sweet poison.

*   *   *

for a word
where there can be no words
a feeling at the source
where they all reside

the dancer
in the hearts of all the ancients
the kiss of the forgotten warrior

yes, that is her abode
her kingdom
her realm
where the golden coins shower upon me
passive illusion
where nothing else
even comes close to mattering

a kiss, oh so passionate
a feeling, oh so strong

nothing even comes close to her embrace
nothing has a chance against her form

and in a world where lies are spoken
it is there where she resides
where the books have no meanings
another illusion
in another mind
her kiss is the strongest
where passion must reside

and in a world
where nothing ever really matters
her embrace is the only one worth seeking

*   *   *

So, we did our shopping session in the abode of creations from other lands and then we moved on and out to my ride again. This time, it was not parked in the strategic W.T. fashion, but instead over to one side.

We sat there for a few. Sat for a few in it; my ride. I, in all of my amazement, was actually allowed to lay my head upon her lap. Her, my *Main L.A. Babe,* has not allowed me to do so in years. Or, at least it seems like years. She, always saying it looked like I was giving her *head.* Something I never did anyway. I mean, *"Uck."* So, it always struck me a funny that she would associate that posture and positioning with such an act.

She always cares what everyone, all the no-ones, think. But, she said nothing today. It just was. Just-was, in a day of just-being.

She said nothing, so I had to say something,

"I shouldn't lay my head here, huh? It looks like I'm giving you head, right?"
"Right!" Very firmly pronounced.

So, I lifted it up, my head, giving her a hot air breath placed and focused directly to her central crotch region.

"How icky," was her statement.
"It is just the one to match the one you laid on the inside of my spectacles inside The Shopping Mall," I replied.

I started the car, and drove on. With tiredness approaching, beingness intact, I headed on down for the ocean. No place left to go and no energy left to shop.

Her car was parked down by my crib. And, though she had wanted to take me to dinner—a rarity within the spectrum of the whole. It usually being I who was the payment factor. But, the space of *Eat* was not at my moment's presence.

I had gotten her a cool antique chest of drawers two days the previous. Though she had thought, I would just pick her up this, *on sale,* white, neo-modern, six-drawer chest of drawers, supplied in part by this W.T. semi-discount major chain department store. Instead, I had gone in and looked at the, *"Advertised Special,"* she had seen and recommended. But, being ashamed to even be within the confines of the walls of said store, I questioned her recommendation. And though and in actuality, it was okay; the chest of drawers. It just did not have any style. Her, my *Main L.A. Babe,* as mentioned, being full on style. It just somehow seemed incomplete/inappropriate to add this piece of *uck* furnishing to her new apartment abode. So me, being the innovative dude that I am, had a flash and I slid on over to an antique store I knew of and picked up this beautiful piece of 1940's furnishing. Hey, I mean, I even delivered it in the back of my open-air Jeep. But, that was two days ago. Thus, so, there-of and there-fore she was going to take me to dinner, tonight.

We hit the parking lot of my crib and the basic game went down as I knew it would, as it always does—was she going to come in or wasn't she?

You see, she is afraid of what may happen in the lust degree if her and I be a-latched up in the zone of tighness within my personal love abode. I told her to forget about dinner for I needed more than she was willing to give me in our contemporary non-existent relationship.

You know, I gave her the typical dude rap.

Not that I really wanted anything. I mean, fuck I had it/her so many times before, I lost count many years ago.

But, you know how it is, you have to play the hand to its fullest, if you catch my meaning. It's like, the babes should all revolve their lives around me, right? We'll, most of them do... They give me what I want, when I want it. While I chill my bones, playing the field. So, it had all become a game between her and I: the have, the have not; the give, the give not.

Told her, *I was burned out, needed emotional sleep.* She said she wanted to take me to dinner even though... And, then she told me that she was just going to go to her relatively near by parent's house, to wait until it was time; my time.

You get the picture etc, etc, etc... She eventually came up and came in, if you know what I be *a-talkin'* about.

*   *   *

We went into my apartment, which actually wasn't in as much disarray, as it generally was. I had been trying to keep things a bit more tidy, if you will.

I sat down on Mr. Couch, turned on the T.V., flipped through the satellite stations. The *Special Report(s)* were still going strong; complete with the aforementioned mid-forties and beautiful Asian commentator.

I was asked to and did so—moved the station, to a little MTV. Some people still don't have it and they, those who don't, somehow seem to assume it holds some rebel enlightenment. It does not.

The main contention for coming up and into my apartment was to take a nap. Did I mention that? Though I, in all honesty, I had the thought of perhaps getting a bit of her physical love potion. I mean it had been awhile since I injected myself into her form.

Let me give you a little background on this. Now, as stated, I had known her, she, my *Main L.A. Babe*, for a lot of years. We meet back in the height of the *Punk/New Wave* days at a nightclub, *Madame Wong's, West*. The almost amusing thing was that I had seen her a week or three before we actually met at another club, *The Starwood.*

I remembered her face, her hair, long and dark brown, her style. That night was the first night that my *L.A. Party Bud,* Saturday Jim, and I had gone to hit the L.A. punk club scene on a serious basis; together that is. Previously, he was into *Country Music. Uck!* Not me! He took me to a Country bar once. Even forced me to wear a cowboy hat. *Double Uck!*

Punk, I had been involved with it/in it long before it was even called *Punk.* Danced with Patti Smith one night at, *The Starwood.* God, I was sixteen.

Dancing with Patti Smith—long before *Punk* was *Punk.* End of the song, she grabbed me, she bit my ear. I smile as I write this. God, that was a long time ago...

You know, just a side note here... Most people weren't there—weren't in it. They either forget or never know how it actually started out. What *"The Look"* really looked like. Back then, when, *The Ramones,* and Patti Smith, changed history.

I mean, the first-wave of the *New Wave,* everybody still had long hair. Dudes would wear their polyester shirts, (ala the Disco Era). They would put tears in 'em. How stupid I thought that was.

Then came the safety pins as earring. Hell, some people even poke them in their face.

Anyway, back to the story... Now there I was a *Punk*—short, spiked hair and all. Somehow though, I had gotten the foolish idea to grow this rather, Frank Zappa looking mustache and under the lip, *soul patch.* To be different and all, you know... Different in the world of *Punk,* where there has never been a stronger sense of ethnocentrism, in any movement, since the Nazis.

But anyway, I stood there, imported beer in hand. She, stood there in all her radiance and beauty. She didn't look *Punk.* No, not all. *New Wave,* maybe a little bit. But, definitely not *Punk.* But, what she was/is very-very beautiful.

That night/then, I tried the casual move in. But, it was *no-wheres-ville Daddy-O.* She didn't dig my scene. So went that evening...

Shaved the *stash*, kept the *do,* the black sport coat, cropped hair, tight black pants, the cockroach killers—seriously pointed red shoes. I mean hey, *The Angel's Want To Wear My Red Shoes* and all.

A few weeks later, there we were, my *L.A. Party Bud,* Saturday Jim and I. Another night, another nightclub, and there she was. She didn't recognize me from before, but I recognized her.

From there is was: love, war, live together(s), (on and off), fights, separations, the entire works. All brought on my me; the asshole who wants 'em all. Promises 'em everything. But, can give 'em nothing. I am hollow. I am empty. I do not feel.

Sometimes you want to make love, sometimes you don't. It is human nature. It is love, boredom, re-love, re-boredom. But we did have an incredible intimacy; she, her and I.

The story, the actually beginning, I believe, goes back way farther than that. We had both spent our early years growing up in not to distant parts of Southcentral. Being the same age, basically, we both used to frequent the same main toy store, over in the far corner of the *Crenshaw Shopping Center.* I am sure/we our sure, our paths must have crossed there. Our vision met early—early on in this life.

*   *   *

A nap, something which I love to do. Funny, most kids never enjoy the full-on intensity, the full-on necessity of a little *siesta* mid-day. Kids become adults and few ever learn to appreciate its art. Me, well I love the realms of sleep. Maybe because I was never forced to take a nap as a kid. No one was around to force me, you know.

Though she was never one who had developed the vision to appreciate the *pure-art* of the nap; she, my *Main L.A. Babe*, was tired too; wanted to crib down on Mr. Couch. Basically, I think to watch the music videos. We had to sit through a few very main stream, very pop ones, by her request,

"You know I don't have MTV, and I like to watch videos." She made that statement.

But, she too was tired and I insisted that she take the bed. I would crib on Mr. Couch. Being the Gentleman that I am...

I offered her my main cool sweat clothing. But, she didn't wish to wear them, for she felt it was too hot. It, being *e.q.* weather and all. So, I loaned her some clothing worthy of her body's sleeping in; my very best short pants: black, long, cuffed and baggy. There is even buttons on the mid side pocket. (Though if you want to put your hands in the pockets you must first unbutton them).

I love refined detail. Like when people take the time to make things really right.

80

Black, well it was her color. For a top, I loaned her a very beautiful green polo shirt. There was a time when I used to wear polo shirts a lot—under a sport coat, of course. Out there on *The Hard Road,* out there in the deep realms of Asia, they are both functional, cool, (in terms of temperature), and they keep you casual while not looking sloppy. But now, mostly they exist within their own space in my closet—never to be worn. But, this one was green, beautiful green. *Green, the most mystical color there is.*

She bailed into the bed, I onto Mr. Couch. I lay there a minute or two and sleep was rapidly upon me. But sleep, at this point, was not the move of intention, not the move in motion.

"I'm lonely, why don't you come and lay in bed with me," I hear in my *Alpha State* vision.

No one, more than I, understood ideologically that we—her and I, should not be making love. We hadn't—had not done the dirty deed for like maybe eight months. She was feeling psychological stigma, due to the bodily insults I had dished her and the generally fucked up person I had been to her over the years. Why she stayed with me, I will never understand...

You know, I've danced with a lot of other women in our, (her and my), time together. Me, well, my illusions were more or less fulfilled, as momentary as desire fulfillment can be, in the lost and distant lands of Asia. I had just recently returned from *Asia Party Central,* where my cup had *runneth* over, if you catch my meaning. Call it desire, with a capital, *"D."* But dude, it doesn't really matter what feminine form you do it with, as long as you do it as much as possible. *'Cause* as the end of the day, that is where all promises and illusions are born, where are the memories are harnessed, and all the basis for literature is found. Shallow, sure, I know.

Anyway, no one understood more than I. Yet, it had been a long time and I looked and I realized that I was/I am harboring all this love in me just ready to come out and flow all over the appropriate female recipient. Her, being the closest one at hand.

It was like this test I gave myself in Indonesia a few years back. I had called up one of the *Jakarta Hilton International,* in-room massage women. Now, in all honesty, I was not quite sure what to expect. I mean some *five-star hotel massage women* are down for the count, while others are there simply to rub out the stress from your hard grind in the international business circuit; world of finance. In my case, this plump little love-muffin arrived, and promptly told be to take off my robe and my boxers. Passion, it was in motion… After a rub or thirty, she gets down to *Dirty Harry* and puts the move on. He rises to the occasion; obviously… Then comes the price.

You know, there is always this bullshit game. First, they get your dick hard and then they spell out the dollars. I mean like, they should just dispense with all of the bullshit, and let's get down to business. I mean, if they are there for insertion, why do they pretend the game to be anything less?

On a funny note, she wanted to sell herself.

"No baby," she said, pointing to her belly. *"Good pussy. Tight,"* she continued.

I smiled. Like, in the middle of this/these situation(s), who the fuck cares?

But, to the point of this little divergence of the storyline. Post the three hundred U.S. dollars agreed upon, (which is/was actually cheap on the Asian hotel fuck side of the photograph), she pulls off her clothing, lies down, grabs a hold of my cock, and literally sticks my dick in her. We get down to business.

I lay there, *missionary style,* doing the dirty deed on top of her. Missionary; she wanted it that way.

I allowed my mind to wonder as I humped on—while the missionary was in motion. I very consciously wondered to that place where the feeling of love emanates from. I allowed myself to feel it; basque in it for a time. Love, I was in love with a chubby, fairly ugly, Indonesian whore. I allowed myself to be in love with her. And, in that place/in that state, I felt all the emotion(s) that were love. Every feeling, it was true/pure. Then she came. Then I came…

*   *   *

I walked in and climbed in bed with her. Her, my *Main L.A. Babe.*

"What are you doing," she asks?

I was a bit set back. Had I been dreaming that statement she had just made as I was roaming through the *ether waves* of the cosmos?

"You said you were going to be a gentleman."

84

"Huh?"

Actually, when it came right down to it, I had offered her the bed due to the fact that all my filing cabinets were in the living room—which, like a magnet she is drawn to; full of all my journals, writings, letters, and other various memorabilia, for my exploits across the globe—L.A. included. Which would have been way inappropriate in her *hot little hands.* I know *'cause,* she has gone searching through them in the past, and her *hot little hands,* got burned.

So, in the bed I get. I snuggle up to her. She gives me the command in Spanish to back off, bail out, *"Ba fueda,"* and to quite suckling in her hair. This being the inside joke between her and I.

You see, a few weeks the previous, I had picked her up this beautiful little kitten at the pricey pet shop in *The Beverly Center.* It had the most intense blue eyes and had just arrived, via special shipment, from Burma. Now, me in Burma, that's another story—another book.

I sure seem to define all my life by my experiences lived in Asia; don't I?

Anyway, she, my *Main L.A. Babe* said, that she just, *"Knew,"* if I purchased the very expensive kitten for her that she would no longer need to make herself throw up after every meal to stay skinny and so on and on and on. Me, being the concerned and caring dude that I am…

In any case, this sweet little feline, having remembrances of her mother, loved to climb into the long flowing hair of her, my *Main L.A. Babe,* as she sleeps and suckle. Which has caused her, my *Main L.A. Babe*, to have to cover her hair at night, with something or other, to keep it untangled and intact.

The kitten, *Kenneth,* named after the shoe designer, because it also has, like her, my Main *L.A. Babe*, a shoe fetish—only the best shoes will do. As it climbs into her shoes to sleep all the time.

Hope, it won't have long lasting psychological problem as it grows up from being left home alone on this L.A. *e.q.* day…

So anyway, I got the basic *negatory* reference in response to my moves *de sexuality*. I, understanding her space, she not feeling my need of contact intimacy. It ended up, I was allowed to lie on the bed, my bed, if no touching were to take place.

Funny, as the story goes… Years before, our first night of official meeting, out in the parking lot of the night club, (you know, where I met her), I give her, my soon to be, *Main L.A. Babe*, the keys to my apartment. She was to drive over to location unknown. This situation occurred, due to the fact, as was virtually the case every weekend, that I had to drive, then carry, my *Party Bud*, Saturday Jim, home to his Hollywood apartment in his general and usual totally intoxicated state. Then, post that endeavor, *(I mean, you can never leave your bros hangin')*, I was to meet her, there at my apartment. Which later became our apartment. I was unusually trusting on my part, if I may say so my self. Me, being the very, *trust no one* sort of person.

That night, our first night, we spoke until the wee hours of the morning; spoke of: music, mysticism, and our early years in Southcentral. Then, we went to sleep on my foam pad of a bed on the floor in the loft section of my apartment. Not touching, not making a move—for every time that I did, her beautiful Spanish eyes would open up in fear of undecided, unapproved slam dances in a unforgotten/unforgiven night.

There we were again, years later, the script was the same. The same gentlemanly refrained from putting the power pup into motion. I silently laughed to myself.

She tells me that it is my temperament to want what I can't have—that's what sends me stroking after every babe I see. Her, now included. Perhaps she is right. I have analyzed it over the several years that she has said this to me and to a degree it is correct. Especially in regard to women. Mostly, I just desire things in the distance—the promise of the illusion. Few, of the things I actually try for, however.

It seems that whatever I go after, really after, be it babes or whatever, I can obtain it. *Remember that projection thing?*

And, I believe everyone is the same. But, so few can acutely focus on what they really want. So, so few ever obtain it. What they want that is...

*   *   *

So, the distance of the desire is better, it holds the illusions. At least it is more stimulating, more debilitating—something to feel upset about.

But then, where is the basis drawn for desire or what is right and wrong? *The cause of suffering is desire.* Where is it said that this is the right desire and that is the wrong desire? Except, of course, what is quoted from some foolish religious text by some late-night cable T.V. evangelists. If it is clear in your own mind and no one is going down hard, then it is AOK. At least, so I surmise.

*   *   *

She says I only want her because she is saying, *"No,"* and that all those times she was there for me, I simply *dised* her, rejected her, cheated on her, and I would do it again if she gave herself to me once more.

Is that true? No doubt...

Perhaps, I too have become lost in the desire. Whatever that desire may be it: love, lust, the new intense infatuations of new love in the distance.

Actually, if I can go into a side note/sidebar here... What else is new; right?

Now, when I dude is *gettin'* ready to hit the road, and he has a main and central babe, what he will do is hit that pussy a lot. Now, the babe generally thinks it is all about love and him wanting to express his love for her in a physical fashion, and shit like that. But, it is not. What it is about is *Practice Sex.*

What *Practice Sex* means is that a dude needs to get his dick *good-and-ready* for the road for, *"The New."* 'Cause when you're out there on *The Hard Road* and you been *a-seekin'* and they, (the felines), be *a-seekin'* you—your dick needs to be ready. You know, just like an athlete works out a lot and gets ready before a competition.

Now, every guy knows, *hittin'* the new and different pussy is exciting. And, if your dick hasn't been in-training, then the session may be over way too fast. If you catch my meaning. And, I know that you do. So, unless you are long-trained in the finer intricacies of *Tantra Yoga,* which I highly recommend, (because it teaches you to hold it forever), then your next best *thAng* is *Practice Sex.* And really, *Practice Sex* is fun. It gives you something to do while you wait for the new out there on the outside/out there on *The Hard Road.*

Anyway, as I lay there this day, I almost felt sad as the realization came to my mind. *"Fuck,"* I thought, *"The amount of times I used her and her body for Practice Sex. Her, my Main L.A. Babe. And, it was all done without her having any knowledge of it—without her realizing it. The amount of times, it is almost unholy..."*

*   *   *

But, then she begins to speak and my mind is shifted from its momentary *head-trip* to what it being dished out at hand...

She tells me I try to manipulate her by buying her things. *"Funny,"* I thought. *"She didn't say that when I took her to Paris and Venice, First-Class, earlier this year. Or,*

90

when I bought her a sports car, when she had crashed her car and needed a new ride, a year or so back."

The truth being told, I love giving people gifts. I desire to make everybody's life better. Not just hers. Obviously, if that ideology were to be analyzed by the proper Freudian psychotherapist, they would surely tell me that this desire was based in my attempting to heal my own psychological wounds inflicted in my childhood. They probably would be right. But, *none-the-less,* it is who I am. I want to give; to help other people have a better life, even when my life is commonly/generally crumbling.

*　　*　　*

As we lay in bed; partially in truth, partially in jest, I say/I ask,

"Why don't you just love me for a little while longer?"
Her answer, *"I can't. I just can't! If I let myself love you again, you will just hurt me again. You will just leave me again. And, this time, I just couldn't take it. I would die."*

in the moments of silence
as we watch the world go by
in the grasp of desire
to be known
to be held
to have anything but nothing
we pay such a high price

and when all the words are spoken
all the stories told
and when there is nothing you can do
to raise the dead
simply kiss the night
kiss the love, once known, good-bye

leave the desire for the living
those who yearn in the night
leave the caress for the moments of motions
when matter has a reason
and caring doesn't possess a name

*   *   *

    Manipulation, desire, psychological pains, control, and scrambled eggs in the morning, they all seem to equal about the same thing—nothing.

We lay there for a while. Her on the ocean side, me on the room side. No touching in progress; as I watched my own misplaced desires: acceptances, forgiveness, understanding, lust. . .

I lay there looking into my mind, focusing/thinking about what I really wanted. What did I really want? Did I want only a little acceptance? Perhaps, a little love? But, then I realized, *No, not love. Not from her. Not from my Main L.A. Babe. No, not any longer. Not from my Main L.A. Babe, who I had known for years, made love with a thousand plus times. Perhaps only a perhaps.*

And then, there was nothing; nothing going up, nothing going down. Somehow, in the beauty of it all, I knew if I simply engaged the nothingness, all would be perfect. I did. It was.

*   *   *

For in all the needs, all the desires, how long do they really last? They are there for a time, and then they are gone. To sit or lay, (as in my present case), in the middle, provides the proof.

One can choose to possess everything, even when there is nothing. Nothing is everything, don't you know?

Even though I momentarily wanted more, I chose to take nothing as an applicable substitute.

I was free. I lay there, simply accepting the situation as it was; feeling nothing, desiring nothing. My mind moved to the clear white light that it has known for so long and *Satori* was embraced.

Emotions are our own choice. They are what we choose them to be.

My eyes were closed. So, I did not see it coming. An *on-coming* hand. It moved its way in my direction. A hand/her hand. Its passage flowed/moved; conceived and received.

Her hand reached over me. It touched my far shoulder. Far away from her.

I don't know, maybe I smiled.

"What are you smiling about," she exclaimed.
"Forget it!" She answered herself.

And, like all women in the mode of play, in the mode of control; it, she, turned it off as fast as it was turned on. But me, desiring nothing, I was free. My eyes remained closed.

"Okay, let's do this!"

I can hear, feel, the shirt I had loaned her coming off. My eyes remained closed.

"Open your eyes, stupid," she said.

My eyes remained closed. She began unbuttoning my shirt. Well, what's a guy like me supposed to do?

I'll skip the small talk and the in-betweens. We got naked. A touch, a kiss, all lost into the pathways of sexual perfection.

My eyes, now opened, studied her body. It was the same body known for so many years. Maybe a bit skinner. She, into all this *hip-and-trendy* anorexia and all. Boobs, a little flabby, a few stretch marks here and there. *But hey, we all get older.* Pussy; bushy—enough to get lost in. Just the way I like *'em.*

I kissed her. I smiled. She smiled. I put my dick deep into her. She obviously felt the powerful insertion. Her large Spanish eyes opened wide.

"Ouh," she said.

Then, as always before, she rolled on top. Did her *thAng.* Came in a few. Rolled her back over. Did my thing. Came. And that, was that.

*   *   *

Perhaps the saddest thing of the long-term love *thAng* is that you get the pattern(s) down. Know what it takes. Do what it takes. We'd done this same thing a thousand times before.

That's why new love is so cool. So there. So, in the moment, I mean like it is all new, all excitement. Finding that place. Defining that *thAng.* But, anyway…

I had got what I had wanted. Even after I didn't care about it anymore. Isn't that always how life is?

*   *   *

The telephone rang. I leaned over the side of the bed and picked it up. It sounded like it was an international call coming in and I thought, *"Oh fuck! How am I going to explain this one?"*

But, I said, *"Hello"* about three times, to no response. My *Main L.A. Babe,* more that jealously curious, I let her listen to the silence, and then I hung up.

"Maybe it was my mother? Do you think it was my mother checking to see if I was okay?"

"Maybe... Or maybe it was one of your China-Doll girlfriends, just hearing about the earthquake on CNN?"

I said nothing. Just left it at that.

She lay there pissed. Slapped hard across the face again.

I could feel her vibes, big time. And, she was right. I felt sorry for her. The mood, any that there was; well it was gone...

I lay there hoping that the phone would not ring again with a distant lover having heard of the L.A. *e.q.* on the other end of line. At least not then, not with my local consort facing the ocean in bed with me.

My mind flashed; realizing again, that I should have moved over Asia way, permanent style—*long-long-ago*. For there, all my dreams are answered and alone never plagued me.

I thought for a second to turn the ringer on the telephone off, but with three telephones in the apartment that would have proven to be a fairly cool trick to perform unnoticed.

A moment or three passed, as we lay in bed. I could feel her eyes burning holes in the ceiling. Then she rolled over. It was sad. Like a poor abused puppy dog, she had once again been beaten with a belt.

Me, I began to wonder who it could have been calling on the international side of the photograph. International, and having my new and continually changing telephone number.

I mean hey, a lot of babes revolve through my life. And, once *you did it,* with most, you just want to *quit it.* So, my number keeps changing…

The only one who came to mind was my *Main Babe in Shanghai.*

Though a bit of anxiety lingered, the telephone did not ring again. A temporal gift from God or my *Spirit Helper,* I believe.

For as much as I love affection, and as much as I love concern, and as much as I wished people had been non-stop calling me this morning—then/there, in bed, with the babe, was not the time for my dreams and desires to be answered.

Funny how desires are… One minute you want *'em;* another you run from *'em.*

She, my *Main L.A. Babe,* was no longer in the mode to sleep. And, after a discussion of the massive beauty of sleeping by the divine mother ocean; she decided it was time to leave, go get our dinner on.

"Not yet, it's too early. Too much traffic. We'll leave at 7:00," I told her.
"What time is it now?"

"6:30."

"You've driven at this time before."

"But there is too much traffic. I want to sleep."

"I don't! Besides, you got what you wanted."

Though she was a hell of an artist, she never did learn the fine art of napping. And, as stated, she just did get slapped—at least to the degree of, *so she felt.* So, we got up.

As to her statement… Yes, the dog in me got what he wanted. Well, kinda. I guess. Maybe. Or not? Actually, I don't think that I really wanted anything.

*   *   *

We got dressed. I watch as her nude body was slowly, precisely covered with clothing. It was an ending. A sad ending.

We headed out and down the stairs to the parking lot below—playing the game of who would drive. As it was a supposed, *"Special Meal,"* being placed in my direction, she won out, as she generally does; I drove.

We got into my Jeep, for its convertibleness; the wind blowing through our hair and all. And, the drive North was on.

I began the subject of talking about how she, my *Main L.A. Babe*, had recently climbed deeply into her own self-misery, and neurosis, and had the seeming inability to climb out.

Me, as neurotic as the best of them, had begun to clean up the picture. The right techniques seemed to be coming my way, undoubtedly at the hands of my *Spirit Helper*. Techniques that took over, where all the years of supposed *Spirituality* had left me cold and unresolved.

She, my *Main L.A. Babe*, a basket case since I met her and I am sure that the proceeding years in this relationship, (or whatever you can call it), had done nothing more than put her deeper in her dilemma, just as it had done to me. So, I put the words on. Telling of *how's* and *why's*. Things that a person, in a less than receptive state of mind, does not wish to listen to, especially from a person who has been less than an excellent example. I mean the best teacher is one who doesn't talk but lives what they be *a-talking* about.

She brought up the facts of this and that; focusing on my faults. I simply explained that,

"I, as her, had a less than idealistic childhood and had a lot of things to work through. More than most."

After continuing on, explaining how I had a lot of my mother's very-negative programming to get out of me, and this works and that doesn't... Then, the word(s) came down,

"Okay, that's enough. I don't want to talk about this anymore."

Instantly, I understood. I was becoming a bit too condescending and a bit too wordy. You know, like all people with Ph.D.s do.

*   *   *

We had agreed for her to take me to dinner on this night, Thursday night. As detailed, it was like a say, *"Thank you,"* session for the cool antique dresser which I had picked up for her.

Two nights ago, she had been working the day; working, and feeling none too righteous. She was a bit ill. I, in fact, had to make excuses that someone might steal the cheap and funky W.T. style *nuevo hip,* from a discount house of a semi major department store, dresser out of my car to get her to let me come over and lay the real *thAng* her direction. She was way far overwhelmed.

Too ill to take me out, to a place of my choosing, and I not being willing to hit the Fairfax food scene, we decided to go for another time/another place. This was it, on an L.A. *e.q.* day; Thursday.

We headed on up to the place I deemed, *"A Special Meal."* One of our main hang outs and go eat kind of places, (almost too frequently), on Wilshire Blvd., in Santa Monica, *Hamburger Henry's.*

I had my heart set on the mean French Onion Soup they put out and a vegetarian style *sang-wich.*

There, I ordered up two of each. Plus, a side of fries, which we could split, and a couple of javas.

The food was good. The eating was better.

There is this strange feeling I have eating with her. It is almost fun. I can't really put my finger on it; as it is something I have just really recently realized—put it down on the metal-mental record, and all. She feels the same. What does it equal? Zero in a zero world...

"You know, today was rather interesting, the people we saw and all," I suggested to her. *"Take for example that interesting little specimen in the warm form of a fuck me doll in the clothing shop today. You know, she really wasn't all that beautiful, nor were her clothing that perfectly picked or placed. It was her more than bitchin' do that made my dick hard and made the difference in her. The same was true for that guy in the Italian clothing store,* (who she, my *Main L.A. Babe,* had creamed over). *Though his hair was pulled back and ponytailed, stylishly tight and his threads were more than well chosen; without them what, would he have been. The clothing or the do are not necessarily the person. Though undoubtedly they do reflect somewhat of the interior."*

"Good," she said, *"I am glad you realize it. Maybe you have learned something new."*

"It is not that I have not realized this before. It was simply once again brought to light in this day lost in desire."

This conversing train of thought went back and forth for a few, as our competitive natures with each other played out their individual parts. Finally, it was laid to rest.

We decided to forego the shared piece of cheesecake we generally consume at this establishment and head on, over, and down to this little, just off of the freeway on Pico, tasty and all-night donut stand, on our way home. Which, by the way, is more than on the bohemian side of the flip side of *thAngs.* Eating donuts and all…

First, though, we were to stroll over, across the street, to this little chain import store—the second import store in one day. But, here/there they have some seriously scented potpourri, that she, my *Main L.A. Babe,* wished to pick up. To chill back the smell of Kenneth. Remember Kenneth?

She paid the bill with her newly arrived AMEX card; moving into and infringing on my turf, the world of plastic passion. Then, we walked across the street.

*   *   *

Noticeable upon on arrival was this man, probably in his early forties. He did have style. I always admire that in a world where so little of it ever exists; so few ever develop it or have the divine intervention of being born with it. The older sets especially, fade so nicely, seemingly so typically, into the acceptable and boring mainstream.

I mean look at the young people; late teens, early twenties; spouting massive excellence in the style *departmento.* Then, time wears on. The mainstream pushes hard and they, they become one of the same, one of the millions, one of the faceless nothings. It's sad I think; style and the lack thereof.

This guy had a cool *do* and was wearing some very chic threads. He had in tow with him a young girl, maybe twelve or thirteen, and a Central American refugee of a maid. I assume the girl to be his daughter.

Oh yes, and by the way—after realizing where his eyes were trained; namely on me, I realized he was quite definitely a serious *ho-mo-sex-u-al*.

Now, the time in the store went by as shopping time does; lost into the pagan worshipping of desireful matters at hands. She, my *Main L.A. Babe*, found her potpourri and assembled just the right amount, (a cupful), into a plastic bag provided by the store to serve just such a function.

Me, I studied these nice little notebooks with Chinese script and images of beautiful Chinese women on the covers— imported directly from Shanghai.

Did I mention what had gone down in Shanghai, with her and me; her, *"The Most Beautiful Woman in Shanghai,"* a few months the previous. No, I did not. Not here, anyway… Another place, another book, another set of circumstances. *Memories, sometimes they kill. . .*

Anyway, the chain import store had some interesting little telephone books, as well. Complete with a little color printed telephone on each section of each page, where the desired phone number should be placed and the imprint of the back of an envelope where the address was to be scribed within; making them a truly international commodity. I thought to, but I didn't, buy one.

The potpourri in hand and a line at the register, with ten minutes to kill before the official closing time of 9:00 PM, we made our way upstairs to the loft of this chain import store where one may find all that is needed in the forms of fine fixtures for the home.

The fag guy was up there shopping for some plates. His probably got broken in the *e.q.*, I thought. Fell out of his cupboards or something.

The little girl was playing with him as he shopped. Obviously, a good father, daughter relationship. However, *ho-mo-sex-u-als* do as *ho-mo-sex-u-als* are, and they have a tendency to check out other dudes way too fully.

Now, what they do is really not my concern. But, it does rather put me off, more than a bit, when I am the unwilling focus of their attentions. I mean negative psychic energy and all.

I guess it's my look, my hair, my multiple and numerous earrings, the clothing I wear. Fuck! I don't know.

I mean like once I was up in Santa Cruz with her, my *Main L.A. Babe*, and I had this really kill sore throat. I always remember back in the day, when I was like thirteen, (way prior to this very common and often taken S.C. trip), and I had the same sort of intense feeling. I mean my throat was kill. It turned out to be a sore throat which went into a respiratory infection. So bad, in fact, I couldn't go teach martial arts for like a week. And, that was my everything back then. I did go, however, walking home from the doctors, as my mother was naturally *en route* to work, you know the story... I went and saw the first theatrical release of a Shaw Brothers, (no relation), film in the U.S., *"Five Fingers of Death."* I mean hey, I had my antibiotics and all...

But, back to the Santa Cruz story... Since then, my childhood, I always worry about way bad sore throats. Anyway, the doctor up S.C. way looked at my throat and then went into this whole discourse about the ill's of homosexuality. As he was the doctor, I listened to him. Said nothing. He then asked me for my telephone number. *If you catch my meaning.* I told him my chick was in the waiting room, waiting for me. He said, *"Oh, sorry. I thought..." "You thought wrong, ass hole."*

But anyway, it is probably how chicks feel when they are not *sluty,* or *scaggy,* or *beachy,* or what ever-else exists in terms, titles, and specification of women who dig being drooled over by whatever male creature may be in sight. But, unless it is a very hot female vixen, *wantin'* me on the serious side of the photograph, I simple do not dig some one digging my scene, especially if they are on the dude side of the picture.

But, being the transcendent guy that I am, I chose not to let it, the *ho-mo-sex-u-al's* check out, control me, and I, went on and about my business of shopping. I mean, I could have, but I didn't, go and blaze the *mutha' fucka* up. Anyway...

I came upon these beautiful bowls under a large sign screaming, *"New Arrivals."* Most were from Japan, some from China. But, they were all beautiful. I proceeded to get the attention of my *Main L.A. Babe* and show them to her. She naturally fell in love with them; being the cultured person that she is.

She also needed to indulge herself with a purchase. A purchased, *physical object of her choosing,* with her plastic money, new AMEX card and all. For somehow my buying her sorrow from her had not completely relieved her pain this day.

We studied the market. Got to know what was available. And, she began to make her choices. I mean like, each individual item has its own specific energy, don't you know?

The initial concept was to get bowls for Kenneth, the kitten. But, beauty soon took hold and the simple became the necessities of desire. She deemed that she also needed a place to offer her daily fruit to the Buddha statue which sits atop a bookshelf in her bedroom.

The Buddha, I had purchased it for her years before, in some foreign land— probably India, I forget. Somehow, I do not quite remember where or when... I must ask her if I ever speak to her again. She, in fact, was the one to remind me of my gift directed towards her salvation many years the previous.

Her Buddha is brass. Mine, however, was plaster-of-paris; purchased in Tijuana, Baja California, Mexico, many years ago. Hers being brass: quietly, meditatively survived the *e.q.* of today. Mine, did not.

But, than nothing is permanent. Certainly
not you or I.

*   *   *

Buddha unleashed his wisdom
it moves forward
onward
wrapped up neatly
in the heart shaped
form of the statue

dense
yet transparent
solid
yet how easily
the Buddha breaks

bleeding Buddha in the blue night
a reminder to time
a reminder to mind
that every rock
has its place
it sits deeply in meditation
as did the Buddha
every rock
speaks to us
of the same truth
truth
that man is too deaf to hear

a rock crumbles
crumbles into sand
religion is believed than lost

we speak of them as ancient
we speak of them as wrong

as the rock crumbles
religions crumble
statues crumble
man crumbles
illusion never was
simply that what we choose to use

truth is not there
no
not there
but here
watch as time crumbles these words
and they forgotten

like all the broken Buddhas
all the religions
that will be lost
all the loves
all the desires
all the nothingness

it is all the same
it is all nothing

*　　*　　*

I came upon this very beautiful bowl and suggested that she purchase it. It had a very beautiful flower design in it.

"Look, isn't this beautiful? This flower is just like the tattoo I have been thinking about getting on my left forearm."
"Oh, then let me buy it for you."
"No, no, no."

This conversation went around in itself/of itself for a time. I finally convinced her that buying it for me would definitely sent me into a new buying binge with bowls at the basis.

*　　*　　*

Bowls are such mystical objects. Now, I am not speaking of the plastic *uck* bowls you can get anywhere/everywhere; mass-produced and all. Though I am not ruling them out, either. For with the right energy all things can find essence. Mostly though, I am speaking of those really unique bowls. The ones that are handmade, hand painted, one of a kind. Their essence is already present. Their truth already apparent.

*   *   *

We, both of us, my Main *L.A. Babe*
and I, have long been into the mysticism of
bowls. So little explanation needed to go on
between us on this subject.

We looked, but that aforementioned
Special One was indeed the only one of its
kind. Subject closed, truth spoken. She was
to buy it for her/herself.

She, my *Main L.A. Babe*, decided to
also get this little three piece set of: two
sake' sized cups and a bowl, as well. All
with the same design as the spoken of bowl,
"Made in China."

It's funny, I guess. Asia always
follows me—like a lost loving kitten or a
spirit in a light green mystical night. It will
never let me go. I can never let her go.

Though my *Main L.A. Babe* saw the
capricho, (Spanish for whim), of it all, I
encouraged her to go for the moment. And
hey, what is life for, but to live out
caprichos.

So, with the flower bowl, the *sake'* set
and, of course, the potpourri in hand, we
made our way down the stairs to the cash
register—ready to pay for the goods.

We stood in line behind the Central
American maid of the *ho-mo-sex-u-al* in
question,   as   the   cashier(s)   unwilling

wrapped two sets of dishes: one blue, one pink. Being it was now a minute or two past 9:00 in the PM, I am sure they, the cashier(s), wanted to bail the scene and head for their own *e.q.* devastated homes. The wrapping, not the *rapin'* continued.

The man, the *ho-mo-sex-u-al,* in question, complete with the little girl, now dressed in a Chinese style hat, was standing at the counter across from us. He kept checking my bones. In an earlier time in my life, he would have been history, his number taken out of the *yellow pages; gratis.* But, I remained calm, even though she, my *Main L.A. Babe,* kept making joking comments to the effect of him digging my scene.

His total came to $200.00 plus. I watched him flinch. He obviously did not have as much style as his *do* and his clothing emulated if he was flinching at that amount. I mean, even if you think it's a lot, you never let on... *Never let 'em see you flinch!*

The number caught him of guard, but he did pay the money.

We too paid our share and bailed for the car.

"So, do you feel better now that you purchased yourself something with you own plastic passion," I inquired.
"Yes," firmly delivered.

"Boy, that dude was in love with you! I could just see the longing, the desire, the lust in his eyes."

"Well, he can go home and pull his pony over me if he wants. Don't you see that's the whole point with people, love, and desire. Just because somebody wants someone, doesn't mean that they can have 'em."

She, my *Main L.A. Babe* continued her jokes for a few. I interrupted her,

"Don't you see, just like I told you today, concerning that semi-fine little Asian princess; people are not something you can buy like a piece of clothing that you like. Even if you do, just like the clothing, the love, the desire, it gets old and you eventually want something new."

Being unduly wordy on this L.A. *e.q.* day, I continued,

"Desire; it is based in control. Desire for control. The more you try to hold it, shape it; the more methods and means you must use to keep it under lock and key. It can make you go crazy. Look at all the ridiculous things I have done trying to control you and your feelings. What was the end result? Disaster. It jut messed you up.

115

Messed me up. Totally fucked over my energy, you know…"

I took a breath. I talked some more…

"That's what love is; desire. That's what lust is; desire. This whole fucking world is based in desire—desire for control. Can't people see there is no control? The more they try, the more it ruins them and everything and everyone else in this universe. Look at toady. There was an earthquake and there was not a fucking thing anyone could do about it! Control, there is no control. People should just let it all go, then they would be so free. But people; people in this world, they are so stupid."
"Okay Mr. Philosopher, that enough."
"Yeah, you're right."

So, we hopped into the ride and drove over and through to the other side of the central city and grabbed us a few donuts. Four, to be exact. *Dos* for me. *Dos* for her.

Though she only wanted to eat one, I insisted that we go for the, *let's gain weight and get fat session.* So, she consumed two.

Ah control; what a fool's game.

We hit back over to my main beach location, yuppie central and all that. She declined the invite that I threw her direction to join me in said premises for a one more time between the sheets session, and she shoved off. Complete with the command that she must telephone me *pronto* if there is any more big *e.q. 's.*

As of yet, there has not been any noticeable *aftershocks* to mention.

I came up here. Here, into my apartment. God, that was a long time ago now. I sat back for a few. Then, got up and ground up some *espresso* blend java beans and brewed up a four-cup amount of the poison in my *cappuccino* machine. I knew it would give me the wire.

I sat back and watched an old episode of, *The Mod Squad.* It must have been made back in '68. '68, the year my father moved on to other realms.

I used to watch it back then. Back in '68. It was one of my favorite shows. I was ten years old. *"One white, one black, one blond,"* and all…

And here; here I am watching it now, all these years later. Late night L.A. T.V. on the cable side of life.

*   *   *

Funny little story here, if I may… Speaking of the, *"One black, one white, one blond."* I met the captain once. The captain of, *The Mod Squad.* It was like a long time ago now—I guess maybe six, seven years back.

I had pulled into an early morning gas station over the San Fernando Valley way. Cruised up in my blue *Krishna* van, *The Dodge Motor Inn,* if you know what I be *a-talking* about. I was pulling in and this guy comes through the driveway in front of me, way cutting me off—almost hitting my ride. He gets out. I was just going to let it go and pulled in on the other side of the pump. But, when I get out to self-service pump the gas; he, this old dude, starts talking shit to me. *"Fuck you,"* I say. With this, the old *mutha' fucka,* he takes a swing at me. Naturally, I blocked it. I mean, not only is this idiot swinging at a young dude, but, fuck, I ran a martial arts studio at the time and I mean come on... I didn't go for the knockout blow; him being an old man and all. I just told him to back the fuck up. About then, out of the passenger side of the ride, gets out the old captain. I told him to hold this guy; obviously his father, back. Or I would put him on the pavement. He said that I had insulted him. *"Fuck you,"* I said, *"He wasn't paying attention and almost ran into my Van."*

That was about it; really. He just told the old guy, in Greek, to calm down and they and me, went about pumping our respective gas. I went up and laid the change on these Mexican employees who had been *watchin'* the situation and were full-on laughing at the whole thing.

No major event, really. Just a minor life story…

I bailed, a bit worried that they, the captain and his father, would get some Greek hit team after me. But, I'm still here today. Well, at least until this book is read. So anyway...

*   *   *

It's light outside now, way light. I have been up all night, writing this tale. There has been a dog barking at some house on *The Strand* for awhile; really annoying… Life in the big city, huh?

But, the waves move to their mystic beat; as they always have, as they forever will; long after I am gone. As they did long before I was here. Someday, I will move into the universe. The same way that a raindrop enters into the ocean. Moving from being one into embracing the whole. And then, perhaps, at some point farther along, a part of what was once my energy will move away from the whole again; evaporate into the atmosphere of everywhere, of singular embrace. And then, only then, someday/ someway to find its way back to being a drop again, and falling once more into the ocean. It'll be like that.

So now, I guess, I will store this little piece of, *for what ever it is worth literature,* on a floppy disk and shut down the computer for the night/for the day.

I think I will go over and give Mr. Buddha a cremation of some sorts. He has been with me many years. But, like all things; nothing lasts forever, certainly not you or I. Then, I think, I will go to sleep for I am tired. It has been a long day/a long night....

S .
1987, 1 October
Redondo Beach, California

120

*   *   *

left to the essence of the unforgiven
that is who I am
cast the realms of the damned
that is where I dwell
shaken to the knowledge
that we are
who we are
we are given
what life has created for us
and that is all
we have to draw upon

so cast me to the goddess
I have lived within her form
cast me to all that is holy
where wholly known
is lost forever

I live
where I live
I dance
where I dance
I live life
the best way
I can live it
      on the edge
      at the source
      at a place
      where most

would never chose to exist

the surcepoint
for all the lust
the home
of all the desire
where creation is formed
and where the living live
the dying die
and most
could never truly survive

welcome to my world

epilogue

A couple of weeks after I wrote this, I was meandering around _The Beverly Center_ and I met a girl. She was/is a beautiful _Glam-Slam_ Asian girl with a cropped leather jacket and red lipstick. Plus, she was/is a complete _Psycho-Bitch._ Just the kind of girl guys like me love. You know, the kind you love to hate. The kind that keeps your dick hard, your blood pressure up, and the adrenaline pulsing through your veins.

In any case, I only saw my _Main L.A. Babe,_ the one mentioned in these pages, a couple of more times after the _e.q._ day in L.A. She was/has been replaced. There's a new, _Main L.A. Babe._

In some ways, I think she, my _Main and Previous L.A. Babe,_ was/is happy for me. For I had found the flavor I was seeking; Asian spiced adrenaline.

For a time, we spoke on the phone; occasionally. Her, my _Main and Previous L.A. Babe,_ and I. That was until me and my big mouth got _a-talkin.'_

I had just come back from Asia and I was telling some sexually explicit, autobiographical story to my bros at the music shop where they customize and make my guitars. I turned around and I noticed somebody else had come into the store and was listening. It was this guy. A *wanta-be* musician.

The problem was, this guy was going out with her, my *Main and Previous, L.A. Babe's,* sister.

From the moment I met that guy, I always though that he was a pussy. I was right.

In any case, the blabbermouth pussy boy went and told her, my *Main and Previous, L.A. Babe,* of what I was *a-speaking.*

I got a call; a message on my message machine, a few days later. A call, telling me, that she, my *Main and Previous L.A. Babe,* was *bailin.'* That she was going to work for the airlines—going to be a waitress in the sky.

"Good for her," I thought. Though I don't have much respect for the profession, I knew it would get her out from behind the ticket selling window at the art museum, (which she didn't really dig), and get her into the, *Friendly Skies.* Mostly, I knew, it would get her away from me.

Finally… She could live her life and maybe she could meet a better man than I. As that sure would not be a hard thing to do.

A side note to the sidebar…

Interesting, I guess, in its own right. Perhaps a bit depictive of this girl, of her mind, and of life in general…

In her farewell address to me, on my answering machine, she never even mentioned all the money she owed me.

You see, since she moved into her apartment, a couple of months before the L.A. *e.q.* day. Which, by the way, was the first time she ever lived alone, ever paid for her own rent. In any case, she had been borrowing a lot of money from me to make ends meet. Every time the gravy train came rolling in, post her begging for it, she would frantically promise to pay me back. I was to be paid someday/sometime. I never really worried or thought about it though. At least not until this point in time. I always figured she get it to me when she got it to me, if she got it to me…

But, with her bailout speech; even thought it was obviously brought on by my actions. You remember, via the rambling mouth of her sister's pussy boyfriend. *I mean a real dude would never give up another of his kind like that.*

Anyway… I had to laugh. I guess the money joke was on me—as it commonly is. Somehow she figured, *"Account Paid in Full."* I don't know how she came to that conclusion, however. But, it was, *none-the-less,* the conclusion she reached.

I guess that's how all women are raised to BE. They just expect the money to be given to them because they are there and *dishin'* out the sex, in the sexual *departmento.*

But really; let's get real—it is not that big of a gift. Hell, if you go out into the *play-a's* world, any dude can get sex, from a different and willing women, everyday of the week; myself included. So, no payment received. No account closed.

In any case, I thought it was funny. Hell, I wish I could take that same road with my bills, my credit cards, my *etcetera...*

I smile as I write this. It was so typical of her. She always was a taker. And, as has always been the case, it seems, I am the one to pay the highest price for my actions/for my choices. Everybody else seems to be able to skate/dance away. But me, I always pay the bill(s) for my indiscretions; her included.

So, that's the story: beginning, middle, and end.

And, as for me... Well, my life ticks *on-and-on-and-on-and-on.*

about the author

Scott Shaw is a prolific author, actor, filmmaker, composer, and photographer. Shaw's poetry and literary fiction were first published by literary journals in the late 1970s. He continued forward to have several works of poetry and literary fiction published, in book form, during the 1980s. By the mid 1980s, after having spent years traveling extensively throughout Asia, documenting obscure aspects of Asian culture in words and on film, his writings on social science began to be published, as well. As the 1990s dawned, Shaw writings, based upon a lifelong involvement with the martial arts and eastern mysticism, began to be embraced. From this, he has authored hundreds of articles and a number of books on meditation, the martial arts, yoga, and Zen Buddhism; published by large publishing houses.

___books by Scott Shaw include:

About Peace: A 108 Ways to Be At Peace
    When Things Are Out of Control
Advanced Taekwondo
Bangkok and the Nights of Drunken Stupor
Cambodian Refugees in Long Beach,
    California: The Definitive Study
Chi Kung For Beginners
China Deep
Essence: The Zen of Everything
Hapkido: Essays on Self-Defense
Hapkido: The Korean Art of Self Defense
Independent Filmmaking:
    Secrets of the Craft
Junk: The Backstreets of Bangkok
Last Will and Testament According to the
Divine Rite of the Drug Cocaine
L.A.: Tales for the Suburban Side of Hell
Marguerite Duras and Charles Bukowski:
    The Yin and Yang of Modern Erotic
    Literature
Mastering Health: The A to Z of Chi Kung
Nirvana in a Nutshell
No Kisses for the Sinner
On the Hard Edge of Hollywood
Sake' in a Glass, Sushi with Your Fingers:
    Fifteen Minutes in Tokyo
Samurai Zen
Shanghai Whispers Shanghai Screams

Shattered Thoughts
Suicide Slowly
Taekwondo Basics
The Ki Process: Korean Secrets for
      Cultivating Dynamic Energy
The Little Book of Yoga Breathing
The Little Book of Zen Mediation
The Most Beautiful Woman in Shanghai
The Passionate Kiss of Illusion
The Screenplays
The Tao of Self Defense
The Warrior is Silent:
      Martial Arts and the Spiritual Path
TKO: A Lost Night in Tokyo
War
Yoga: The Spiritual Aspects
Zen Buddhism: The Pathway to Nirvana
Zen Filmmaking
Zen in the Blink of an Eye
Zen O'clock: Time to Be
Zen: Tales from the Journey

www.ingramcontent.com/pod-product-compliance
Lightning Source LLC
Chambersburg PA
CBHW060400090426
42734CB00011B/2205